A Manual for Clergy and Church Musicians

A Manual for Clergy and Church Musicians

Prepared by Marion J. Hatchett

for The Standing Commission on Church Music

The Church Hymnal Corporation
800 Second Avenue, New York, N Y 10017

Acknowledgements

This manual was prepared at the request of The Standing Commission on Church Music, which then reviewed and edited the manuscript. In the following revised form it has been accepted by the Commission as the consensus of its members. Special mention should be made of the contributions of James H. Litton, especially to the lists of recommended music, and of Joyce Glover (Mrs. Raymond F.) who typed and copy edited the manuscript.

Contents

Introduction

Part One: Musical Ministries

Appendix I:

Appendix II: Check Lists for Planning Services

Appendix III:

Abbreviations

The following are abbreviations used in the text for publications of The Church Hymnal Corporation:

BC	The Book of Canticles
BCP	The Book of Common Prayer
BOS	The Book of Occasional Services
CHS I	Church Hymnal Series I: Five Settings of the Common Texts of the Holy Eucharist
CME	Congregational Music for Eucharist
GPAVT	Gradual Psalms, Alleluia Verses and Tracts
HEAE	The Holy Eucharist: Altar Edition
MMC	Music for Ministers and Congregation
MMC II	Music for Ministers and Congregation II
MNOC	Music for the Noonday Office and Compline
MOWE	Music for An Order of Worship for the Evening

Introduction

Role of music in the Church. From the early days of the Church, music has been integral to the worship of God. Music gives solemnity, beauty, joy, and enthusiasm to the worship of the community. It imparts a sense of unity and sets an appropriate tone for a particular celebration. It is an effective evangelistic tool. It nourishes and strengthens faith and assists worshipers in expressing and sharing their faith. It heightens texts so that they speak more fully and more cogently. It highlights the basic structure of the rites. It expresses and communicates feelings and meanings which cannot be put into words. As Messiaen expressed it, "The joy of music is that it can go beyond words—which are too precise. Music can express what there is in the soul."* Music however must not dominate the liturgy; all elements of liturgy must work in harmony. Music, and the other arts, including speech, serve together in the liturgical action.

Music is not necessarily helpful in a service. It can, in fact, be destructive of a rite. This is the case when music is used for its own sake or only as a demonstration of the virtuosity of the performers, when it is

*NEWSWEEK, *November 23, 1970, page 139*

beyond the abilities of the performers, when it interferes with the basic movement of the rite, when it gives undue prominence to secondary elements in a rite, or when the mood is out of keeping with the day or occasion.

Music should serve to set a tone, to convey texts, to highlight basic structures, to unify the congregation, to express the highest possible excellence. An appreciation of the proper relation of music and of other arts to the liturgy must be sought and developed if the Church is to resume a major role as patron of the arts.

The Canon: Of the Music of the Church. It is imperative for clergy, musicians—in fact, for all liturgical planners—to "read, mark, learn, and inwardly digest" the present canon of the music of the Church.

Title II, Canon 6, Of the Music of the Church, Section I, reads:

It shall be the duty of every Minister to see that music is used as an offering for the glory of God and a help to the people in their worship in accordance with the Book of Common Prayer and as authorized by the Rubric or by the General Convention of this Church. To this end the Minister shall have final authority in the administration of matters pertaining to music. In fulfilling this responsibility the Minister shall seek assistance from persons skilled in music. Together they shall see that music is appropriate to the context in which it is used.

These last two sentences date from the General Convention of 1976, replacing these lines:

To this end he [*the Minister*] *shall be the final authority in the administration of matters pertaining to music, with such assistance as he may see fit to employ from persons skilled in music. It shall be his duty to suppress all light and unseemly music and all irreverence in the rendition thereof.*

Provisions for music in the Prayer Book. The emphasis on music is heightened in the new edition of THE BOOK OF COMMON PRAYER. Much that had been assumed is now verbalized. Music has a larger place in many of the rites. Specific directions appear for its use in many situations not dealt with in general directions or in the rubrics of previous editions of THE BOOK OF COMMON PRAYER.

In the section "Concerning the Service of the Church" (pp. 13-14) four paragraphs deal with general directions concerning music:

> *Hymns referred to in the rubrics of this Book are to be understood as those authorized by this Church. The words of anthems are to be from Holy Scripture, or from this Book, or from texts congruent with them.*
>
> *On occasion, and as appropriate, instrumental music may be substituted for a hymn or anthem.*
>
> *Where rubrics indicate that a part of a service is to be "said," it must be understood to include "or sung," and* vice versa.
>
> *When it is desired to use music composed for them, previously authorized liturgical texts may be used in place of the corresponding texts in this Book.*

It is important to note that these paragraphs take the place of a rubric included in the 1892 and 1928 editions:

> *Hymns set forth and allowed by the authority of this Church, and Anthems in the words of Holy Scripture or of the Book of Common Prayer, may be sung before and after any Office in this Book, and also before and after sermons.*

The texts of anthems are no longer limited to words of Holy Scripture or THE BOOK OF COMMON PRAYER; "texts congruent with them" may also be used. The general permission to utilize hymns or anthems before and after any rite or sermon has been withdrawn. Such uses are often antithetical to the text of the rites (for example, a hymn prior to the Opening Preces of Morning Prayer ["Lord, open our lips"] or after the Dismissal at the Eucharist ["Go in peace. . . . ."]). Hymnody should not interrupt the movement from the Readings to the sermon or from the sermon to the Creed or Prayers. In its rubrics for individual rites or in the directions appended to the rites, this new edition of the Prayer Book designates points for appropriate use of hymns or anthems.

The word "hymn" as used in the rubrics of the Prayer Book refers to a congregational song whose text is currently authorized. "Hymn" is used consistently in the rubrics of the Daily Offices, the pastoral Offices, the episcopal services, and the Holy Eucharist: Rite One and Rite Two. In An Order for Celebrating the Holy Eucharist (pp. 400-401), however, the more inclusive word "song" appears. The text of a "song" need not have current authorization. The word "anthem" in the rubrics refers to music sung by the choir rather than by the congregation.

This is the first edition of THE BOOK OF COMMON PRAYER to mention the use of instrumental music in the rites. It explicitly suggests instrumental music as an alternative to a hymn, psalm, or anthem at the entrance and exit of a wedding party (pp. 423 and 432) and during the procession and after the dedication of a musical instrument in the rite for the Consecration of a Church (pp. 567 and 572). "On occasion, and as appropriate" instrumental music may be substituted for a hymn or anthem in other rites.

The new BOOK OF COMMON PRAYER gives general permission either to say or sing any text. There is no historic basis for the late Victorian idea that it is only proper to say certain texts and to sing others. In the Eastern Church and in the medieval "high mass" the entire text heard by the people was sung. Merbecke's BOOKE OF COMMON PRAIER NOTED (1550) provided music or musical directions for almost the whole text of the Eucharistic rite, including the Prayer for the Church and the Eucharistic Prayer. The acoustics of the building, the ability of the various participants, the taste of the congregation, and the relative importance of the day or occasion, rather than any canons of proper procedure, should determine what is said and what sung.

The last of the general musical directions gives explicit permission, when using music composed for them, to use previously authorized liturgical texts in place of the corresponding texts of the new BOOK OF COMMON PRAYER. Since 1789 the American texts of the Te Deum laudamus and the Benedicite, omnia opera Domini have been different from those in the English Prayer Books. On occasion it may be desirable to use music composed for the English versions of these canticles. It may also, at times, be advantageous to use earlier versions of various other forms, especially when the earlier version is in the hands of the congregation or when the music cannot be adapted easily to the revised text.

Uses of silence. Prior editions of THE BOOK OF COMMON PRAYER specifically directed silence at only one point, in the ordination of a priest. The new edition suggests silence at many other points including: after the Readings, before General Confessions, immediately before the Collect of the rite, during the Breaking of the Bread. Silence is creative and has its own validity. Silences allow for recollection (as before Confessions or Collects) or for reflection (as after the Readings and during the Breaking of the Bread). Additional silences would often be appropriate, for example, before and/or after the sermon and prior to the Eucharistic Prayer or the postcommunion prayer. Actions do not always need musical accompaniment. The new BOOK OF COMMON PRAYER explicitly directs that the Bread be broken in silence. The organist must resist the temptation to fill every silence with sound. An improvisation is often unneeded between prelude and entrance hymn or between Offertory anthem and Sursum Corda; a period of silence is often much more effective. Until a congregation becomes accustomed to silence and does not interpret it as a missed cue, periods of silence should be noted in the service sheet. The liturgical planners in a congregation should assume an active role in teaching the meaning and uses of silence.

PART ONE:

Musical Ministries

In all services, the entire Christian assembly participates in such a way that the members of each order within the Church, lay persons, bishops, priests, and deacons, fulfill the functions proper to their respective orders, as set forth in the rubrical directions for each service.

This principle, set forth in the section, "Concerning the Service of the Church" (p. 13), of THE BOOK OF COMMON PRAYER, is true for the music as well as for the other aspects of the worship of the Church. The Church's tradition, and the rubrics of the new edition indicate that certain functions belong to lay persons, others to bishops, others to priests, and others to deacons. Furthermore, by tradition (and frequently by rubric) certain musical portions of the rites are reserved for the people. Other musical elements of the rite are properly performed by choirs, by cantors, or by instrumentalists.

The Musical Ministry of the People

The songs of the people. The rubrics of the new BOOK OF COMMON PRAYER are true to tradition in reserving for the people the responses to the Opening Acclamation, the Salutation, the acclamations at the beginnings and endings of Lessons, responses in the Prayers of the People, the response to the Peace, responses in the introductory dialogue of the Eucharistic Prayer, and the response to the Dismissal. The Amen, wherever it occurs, belongs to the people. The Kyrie and the Trisagion are songs of the people. The Sanctus and Benedictus qui venit, the Memorial Acclamation, and the Lord's Prayer are songs which the people sing along with the celebrant. The word *hymn* is used in the rubrics to indicate a metrical song of the people. In other rites, as well as in the Eucharist, certain portions are reserved for the people as, for example, the responses to the Opening Preces and the Suffrages in the Daily Office. The Apostles' Creed and the Lord's Prayer are songs which the people and celebrant sing together. It is highly inappropriate for these portions of the rite to be preempted by a choir. These portions belong to the people; unless the congregation can sing them easily, they should say them. Music too complicated for the congregation should not be used for these portions of the rites. A church music director desiring to perform a more complicated setting of one of these texts (for example, the Sanctus) should do so either at a time within the service appropriate for an anthem or at a concert. In early Anglicanism the more elaborate settings of the Sanctus were used, not within the Eucharistic Prayer, but rather as an introit for the rite. Often the Sanctus within the Prayer was said or sung to a simple setting, so important was congregational participation in the historic songs of the people.

In addition to those portions of the rites reserved to the people, traditionally the congregation sings hymns or canticles as a part of the entrance rite; the response in the Gradual Psalm (or the Psalm itself); the Alleluia, Psalm or Sequence hymn prior to the announcement of the Gospel; the Nicene Creed; the Fraction Anthem; and possibly hymns or psalms during the preparation of the Table, during the Communion of the People, and before or after the postcommunion prayer. In the Daily Office it is traditional for the people to sing the Invitatory Psalm, the Psalmody of the Day, and the Canticles, or to sing antiphons when a cantor or choir sings the aforementioned portions of the rite.

The function of the songs of the people. The aim of the songs of the people is that "full, conscious, and active participation . . . demanded by the very nature of the liturgy" (*The Constitution on the Sacred Liturgy,* 14).

Though music may add solemnity, effectiveness, beauty, enjoyment, and unity to a celebration, that is not always true. It is not always better to sing than to say; silence is to be preferred at times to sound. It is essential to consider the particular gathering of people, the size of the group, their traditions, their musical abilities, the available musical leadership, the architectural setting, and the relative importance of the day or occasion. Also important are the predominant age group, the degree of experience with a particular service, and the musical interest of the particular gathering. The music must not dominate the rite but instead highlight its basic structure.

The Musical Ministry of the Cantor, Song Leader, or Clerk

The functions of the cantor. A fourth century practice still maintained in large portions of the Church today is to have a soloist sing the Gradual Psalm, the Alleluia Verse at the Eucharist, and the Invitatory Psalm (Venite or Jubilate Deo) at the Daily Office. In the Gradual Psalm the cantor sings first a refrain enunciating the theme of the Psalm or setting forth its application to the day or occasion. The choir and congregation then repeat the refrain and sing it at subsequent appropriate intervals throughout the Psalm. (See GPAVT.)

The cantor initiates the Gospel Acclamation by singing the Alleluia(s) which is then repeated by the choir and congregation. The cantor then sings the Verse, after which the choir and congregation repeat the Alleluia(s). (See GPAVT.)

The Invitatory Psalm at the Daily Office may be treated in the same manner as the Gradual Psalm, making use of the Invitatory Antiphons as refrains. (See BC.)

In addition to the Gradual, the Alleluia, and the Invitatory Psalm, other psalms or hymns with refrains may be very effective if sung by a cantor, with congregational refrains, at the entrance of the ministers, during the Offertory procession or during the Communion of the People. Sometimes a cantor can effectively initiate the Memorial Acclamation, the Fraction Anthem, or even the Sanctus and Benedictus qui venit. With shorter texts, such as the Kyrie, the Trisagion, the Memorial Acclamation, or the Fraction Anthem, it is often effective for the cantor to sing the whole text or a section of it after which the celebrant, the choir, and the people repeat it.

By singing new music as a solo on several occasions, the cantor can be very helpful in teaching new music to the congregation. Also, the cantor might lead a rehearsal before the service, or, on occasion, within the rite at a time for announcements or some other appropriate time.

In some situations it is both more desirable and practicable to use a cantor for those portions of the rites normally sung by choirs than to attempt the development of a choir. In situations where the instrument and/or the skills of the instrumentalist are limited, the cantor can often provide the necessary leadership.

The qualifications of the cantor. Because of the functions of the cantor, it is important that this person have a pleasant voice; a commanding presence; and the ability to read music accurately, to learn music with ease, and to sing with confidence. The cantor must also be able to present ideas clearly and briefly. The procurement of an able cantor would greatly enhance the musical performance in many churches. Even churches with limited budgets should think seriously about hiring a cantor if a talented volunteer is not available. This person could be either male or female.

The Musical Ministry of the Choir

The function of a choir in the rites of the Church is not that of a choral society or a glee club. In the last two groups the music brings the people together, and their principal purpose is to provide an opportunity to practice and perform music which cannot be performed individually. A choral society or glee club performs publicly for the edification and enjoyment of others and for their own gratification. Although these same functions may be served by the church choir, they must be subservient to the role of music within the liturgy of the Church.

Types of choirs. Each congregation should decide whether a choir is desirable for it, and, if so, what type of choir or choirs. In some situations, the formation of a choir would necessitate gathering from the congregation all those who sing with confidence, thereby robbing the congregation of leadership and support needed in their midst.

(1) The cathedral or collegiate choir. In some situations a cathedral or collegiate choir is both possible and appropriate. In the traditional cathedral or collegiate situation the choir is the congregation; the chancel serves as the church or chapel for the services. (The nave is the

place for occasional visitors, but essentially the choir is the congregation and the congregation is the choir.) In many ways the cathedral or collegiate situation is analogous to a congregation with no choir. The difference lies in that the daily services in the cathedral or collegiate situation include music, and in the ability of the regular congregation to perform music not within the capability of a typical congregation. Historically, it was in the former situations that a divided choir was to be found. Since antiphonal psalmody was basic to the repertoire, the divided choir was functional. Today where the choir and congregation are essentially the same (as in some seminary chapels, monasteries or convents, and in occasional American cathedrals and school chapels), it is certainly appropriate to make use of highly complicated service music which, in other situations, might obscure the liturgy.

(2) The parish choir. The parish choir and most cathedral and collegiate choirs must take seriously the presence of a congregation which neither practices nor sings together with great frequency. These choirs must recognize their primary function to be that of providing leadership, support, modeling, and teaching for those of more limited musical aptitudes and abilities. Many congregations include a sufficient number of children and adults with musical interests and abilities to comprise a choir. In some parishes the choir of volunteers is sufficiently talented to provide music beyond the talents of the congregation. In some situations even two people could be the choir. In other situations it is necessary to pay a certain number of trained singers to fill particular needs or to provide the backbone for the larger volunteer group. Just as a church must often pay for the time and talents of clergy, secretaries, sextons and others vital to the proper functioning of the congregation, so it must be willing to pay for the time and talents of persons with musical abilities to provide leadership and enhance the program of the parish choir.

In a cathedral or parish choir it is sometimes possible, or even desirable, to have a small group of people with extraordinary time and talents devote themselves to performing highly complex music beyond the time and abilities of the entire choir. This select group might take the place of a cantor or choir at appropriate points in the rites.

(3) The young people's or children's choir. A children's choir can make its own contributions. It can sing alone and, on occasions, sing

with an adult choir as well as provide a training school to feed into the adult choirs. The young people's choir and the children's choir both provide an excellent opportunity for education in the liturgy and music of the Church. Because they have not been negatively acculturated, young people or children are often able to learn music such as plainchant much more easily than adults and then to initiate its use in a congregation. In many places a young people's or children's choir could be the only choir; the combination of cantor and young people's or children's choir might be ideal.

(4) The ad hoc choir. In many congregations people who do not have time or interest sufficient for involvement in the regular choir(s) can augment the choir for certain special events or compose a choir for certain functions. Because the members of the regular choir(s) are often busy at the times of weddings and funerals, many churches have compiled lists of persons available to form a choir when desired. Since regular service music and a few well-known hymns generally make up the repertoire for weddings and burials, an ad hoc choir can often contribute effective leadership after only a brief practice just prior to the rite.

The functions of choirs. Of primary importance to the church choir is its role as leader, supporter, and teacher of the congregation in the songs of the people and in unison reading and as model and teacher for the congregation in good liturgical and worship habits. Any choir failing to understand the significance of these roles may be of more detriment than help in the worship of the church. A substantial portion of many choir practices should be devoted to the study of liturgy, unison reading, and the practice of the songs of the people so that the choir may better perform its primary functions. In addition to these, the choir may be able to provide other rite-enhancing elements, beyond the abilities of the congregation.

The choir may also enhance songs of the people and hymns which the congregation sings with confidence by supplying harmony, descants, or faux-bourdons. Caution must be exercised, however, lest such variations discourage the singing of the people. Among the available collections containing descants, or faux-bourdons, the following are especially valuable:

The Christ Church Descant Book. Fyfe, Lois, Cumberland Press.

The Descant Hymn-Tune Book, *Books I & II.* Shaw, Geoffrey, Novello.

Familiar Hymns with Descants. Kettring, Donald, Westminster Press.

Festival Praise. Routley, Eric, Hinshaw Music.

Hymns for Choirs. Willcocks, David, oup.

Thirty-four Hymn Descants. Williams, David McK., H.W. Gray (Belwin-Mills).

Thirty-six Descants. Shaw, Geoffrey, oup.

20 Hymn-Tune Descants. Lang, C.S., Novello.

Often the choir may take the place of the cantor in singing the text of the Gradual Psalm or the Alleluia Verse at the Eucharist or in singing the text of the Invitatory Psalm at the Daily Office. On occasion it is also appropriate for the choir to sing certain portions of the rites often sung by the people; i.e., the Gloria in excelsis at the Eucharist or a canticle at the Daily Office. The rubrics state that an anthem may be used at the place of the Gradual or of the Alleluia Verse at the Eucharist. The functions of these components of the rite must be carefully considered in the choice of anthems. Some of the early Church Fathers referred to the Gradual as the Lesson from the Psalms. The Alleluia is an acclamation at the appearance of Christ present in his Word, symbolized by the Gospel Reading. It is common for the choir to sing the Fraction Anthem (in fact, the new Prayer Book uses the word *anthem* rather than *hymn* at this place in the rite) to afford opportunity to the people for concentration on the liturgical action. It is traditional in Anglicanism for an anthem to follow the Collects of the Daily Office.

The songs of the choir. From the fifth century the songs traditionally assigned to the choir have been the three processional songs of the Eucharistic rite: the entrance song, the Offertory song, and the Communion song. Other musical portions are integral to the rite, and the texts are normally read when they are not sung. These processional songs serve primarily to accompany actions and are not essential to the actions. Traditional liturgies have assigned the music at the three processions to the choir so that the people might be free to take part in the procession or to watch it in progress.

In classic liturgies the entrance song, which sets the mood for the rite, was assigned to the choir who sang only that portion of a psalm needed for the entrance of the ministers. Hence, the Gloria Patri at the end provided a climax and a cue to the celebrant to be ready to start. Throughout most of Anglican history, however, a congregational hymn has replaced this choir anthem. The Trial Liturgies listed a psalm as the first option at this point, but in response to popular request, the new BOOK OF COMMON PRAYER restored the hymn to primacy here. If the people sing the entrance song, it is certainly legitimate or even desirable on occasion for the choir to sing the Gloria in excelsis or another song of praise in its place. It is probably wise for the congregation to sit during the choir's singing of the song of praise, especially if it is lengthy. Then the people stand again at the Salutation.

The Offertory song serves to accompany the preparation of the Table and the presentation of the bread and wine and money or other offerings. As at the entrance, the needed portion of an appropriate psalm was sung with the ending indicated by the Gloria Patri. Music used at this point in the rite should serve as a meditative aid to the congregation in its preparation for participation in the Great Thanksgiving. The music should not overshadow the songs of the people within the Eucharistic Prayer.

The Communion song is the third of the processional songs traditionally assigned to the choir. Anthems too lengthy or too dramatic for use at the preparation of the Table are often suitable at this point. Responsorial psalms or hymns or anthems which include refrains work well at this time for they enable the congregation to participate without being bookbound.

In addition to its function within the liturgical rites, the choir may make an offering to God and serve the church through special services with music possibly not suited for use in liturgical rites. Concert masses, oratorios, cantatas, services of lessons and music (especially those associated with the Advent and Christmas Seasons), and para-liturgies (services created for various seasons and occasions) are rich resources for such special musical offerings. Often singers and instrumentalists not available for the regular Sunday and Holy Day Eucharists or for the Daily Office can augment the regular choir.

The location of the choir. During the late nineteenth and early twentieth centuries many Anglican parish churches forsook the traditional west end gallery position for the parish choir. Because of a misunderstanding of the makeup and function of the cathedral or collegiate choir, many churches in building or remodeling created a chancel placement for the choir (often divided into two sides). The resultant separation of the clergy from the people had harmful effects on the liturgy. Also, the choir was less able to give effective leadership to the people. Happily, with the building of new churches and many remodelings of existing buildings, we now see a return to the traditional western choir placement in a gallery or in the back of the church or to the traditional eastern position among the people in the nave (possibly slightly raised above the nave floor). Each position has its own distinct advantages. Some churches, when remodeling, have found it best to reverse the placement of the choir and sanctuary, placing the organ and choir in the old sanctuary facing the people, and using the old choir area as the place for altar and pulpit. Thus the united choir can provide better leadership for the people. In turn, the people are better able to see and feel involved with the actions at the principal liturgical centers.

Facilities for choir practice. Although a frequent final rehearsal in the church is helpful, the choir should not be forced to do all their preparation there. A well-arranged choir room can greatly facilitate rehearsals and save an appreciable amount of time. The room should be spacious and well-ventilated. Absolutely essential is a good piano placed so that the director faces the choir. The room should be isolated from other activities and free before services to allow for a brief warmup. Essential equipment includes: chairs with book racks; book shelves and filing cabinets or other storage facilities for hymnals, Prayer Books, anthems, and other music; and a chalk board, probably with a section lined with music staves. A large wall clock facing the director facilitates the best use of time. A bulletin board and a tape recorder and/or turntable are helpful.

Vestments. In medieval cathedral or collegiate churches the members of the choir wore the clerical vestments appropriate to their order. This vestment was often a quite full form of the ankle-length alb known as the *surplice* ("over the fur," for this full form could be worn in unheated buildings over an overcoat, often in the form of a cassock). After the Reformation the young scholars, taking the place of eliminated minor orders, continued to wear the clerical surplice in choir. Those in parish choirs generally wore no special vestments. About the turn of this century an unattractive abbreviated version of the surplice, known as a *cotta*, appeared in many places, but currently there seems to be something of a return to the more traditional fuller and longer form. Many churches have found a simple robe modeled after the academic gown more practical as it is easier to keep clean and fresh and is also more comfortable. It is not necessary, and probably not even desirable, to wear a headcovering with vestments. In situations where the choir is located behind the people, vestments are often considered more of a nuisance than a help. Some of these churches have returned to the tradition of the unvested parish choir, although other churches still find vestments an aid to morale.

Music. The inflated cost of anthems and larger choral works has in recent years put quite a strain upon many music budgets. In many areas choirs are able to exchange catalogues of their music libraries and then borrow from each other. The new music included in THE BOOK OF CANTICLES and HYMNS III is a tremendous resource for choirs. This music performed as anthems serves to familiarize the people with music which they can eventually sing as songs of the people. THE HYMNAL 1940 is still a usable resource for choir music. Later in this book appear hints on how to add interest for the choir as well as the congregation when using a hymn or canticle as an anthem.

The following collections contain multipurpose, high quality anthems:

Anthems for Choirs Book i. (ed. Francis Jackson) 4 part choirs, oup.

Anthems for Choirs Book ii. (ed. Philip Ledger) unison & 2 part choirs, oup.

Anthems for Choirs Book iii. (ed. Philip Ledger) 3 & 4 part treble choirs, oup.

Anthems for Choirs Book iv. Compiled by Christopher Morris, mixed choir, oup.

The Oxford Book of Tudor Anthems. (ed. Christopher Morris) oup.

Carols for Choirs, 1, 2, 3. (ed. David Willcocks, Reginald Jacques, and John Rutter) oup.

Oxford Easy Anthem Book. oup.

Sixteenth Century Anthem Book. oup.

The Church Anthem Book. oup.

The Chester Book of Motets. (ed. Anthony G. Petti) 6 volumes, oup.

The Oxford Book of Carols. oup.

Motet Book i, ii. Concordia.

SAB Choir Goes Baroque. Concordia.

16 Hymns of Today for use as Simple Anthems. (ed. John Wilson) rscm.

Bach for Choirs. (ed. Paul Steinitz) rscm.

Six Easy Three-Part Anthems, SAB. (ed. A. Greening) rscm.

Twelve Easy Anthems. rscm.

Five Anthems for Today. rscm.

Anthems from Addington. rscm.

Anthems for Unison or Two-Part Singing. rscm.

Churches must resist the temptation to duplicate music under copyright. Copyright laws make it legitimate to reproduce portions of works of music for classroom purposes and to reproduce certain music no longer available for purchase. However, it is not legitimate to reproduce for performance entire copies of available anthems or other works under copyright. The basic principle seems to be that music may not be reproduced if that reproduction interferes with sales.

Guidelines for educational uses of music.* The purpose of the following guidelines is to state the minimum and not the maximum standards of educational fair use under Section 107 of H. R. 2223. The parties agree that the conditions determining the extent of permissible copying for educational purposes may change in the future; that certain types of copying permitted under these guidelines may not be permissible in the future; and conversely that in the future other types of copying not permitted under these guidelines may be permissible under revised guidelines.

Moreover, the following statement of guidelines is not intended to limit the types of copying permitted under the standards of fair use under judicial decision and which are stated in Section 107 of the Copyright Revision Bill. There may be instances in which copying which does not fall within the guidelines stated below may nonetheless be permitted under the criteria of fair use.

A. Permissible Uses

1. Emergency copying to replace purchased copies which for any reason are not available for an imminent performance, provided purchased replacement copies shall be substituted in due course.

2. For academic purposes other than performance, single or multiple copies of excerpts of works may be made, provided that the excerpts do not comprise a part of the whole which would constitute a performable unit such as a section, movement or area, but in no case more than (10%) of the whole work. The number of copies shall not exceed one copy per pupil.

*COPYRIGHT HANDBOOK, *Donald F. Johnston. R.R. Bowker Co.*

3. Printed copies which have been purchased may be edited or simplified, provided that the fundamental character of the work is not distorted or the lyrics, if any, altered, or lyrics added if none exist.

4. A single copy of recordings of performances by students may be made for evaluation or rehearsal purposes and may be retained by the educational institution or individual teacher.

5. A single copy of a sound recording (such as a tape, disc or cassette) of copyrighted music may be made from sound recordings owned by an educational institution or an individual teacher for the purpose of constructing aural exercises or examinations and may be retained by the educational institution or individual teacher. (This pertains only to the copyright of the music itself and not to any copyright which may exist in the sound recording.)

B. Prohibitions

1. Copying to create or replace or substitute for anthologies, compilations or collective works.

2. Copying of or from works intended to be "consumable" in the course of study or of teaching, such as workbooks, exercises, standardized tests and answer sheets and like material.

3. Copying for the purpose of performance, except as in A(1) above.

4. Copying for the purpose of substituting for the purchase of music, except as in A(1) and A(2) above.

5. Copying without inclusion of the copyright notice which appears on the printed copy.

Training of Choirs. Even the smallest choirs with the most inexperienced directors can improve their ability to lead congregations in the liturgy. There are a large number of books, booklets and pamphlets, workshops, seminars and conferences as well as recordings which demonstrate and illustrate concepts of choral techniques, including breathing, good tone, rhythmic singing, blend, balance, interpretation, etc.

Many diocesan liturgical and music commissions sponsor weekend workshops for directors and choir members, and the summer months provide numerous opportunities for workshops and seminars at colleges and universities. The Standing Commission on Church Music often sponsors workshops on the relation of music and the liturgy and each summer the Sewanee and Evergreen Conferences provide large numbers of church musicians with new choral skills and a deeper understanding of the relation of music to the liturgy.

Some important choral training books include:

CHORAL DIRECTING. Wilhelm Ehmann, Minneapolis, Augsburg, 1968.

THE CHURCH CHOIR TRAINER. Henry Coleman, London, OUP, 1964.

BASIC CHOIR TRAINING. Edward Wright, Croydon, RSCM, 1953.

CHORAL CONDUCTING — A SYMPOSIUM. Hurford and Becker, Prentice Hall.

Also helpful are the Adult and Childrens' choirs Training School booklets and the self-help booklets published by the Royal School of Church Music.

The Musical Ministry of Directors and Instrumentalists

Functions of directors and instrumentalists. Often one person is both director and instrumentalist, but even if several different persons perform these tasks, the functions still overlap. The director or instrumentalist is first of all a teacher and a leader; all other roles are secondary.

(1) A teacher. The director or instrumentalist is a teacher of the people, of the choir, and of the clergy. This person should know thoroughly the contents of THE BOOK OF COMMON PRAYER, THE HYMNAL 1940, the CHURCH HYMNAL SERIES, THE HOLY EUCHARIST: ALTAR EDITION, and MUSIC FOR MINISTERS AND CONGREGATION. This person has not only

primary responsibility for teaching the people hymns, canticles and service music but also the opportunity to teach the Prayer Book and to engender good worship habits. The director or instrumentalist can teach the choir in even greater depth and wider compass. This is the person to introduce new music to the clergy and to coach them in singing their parts of the rites.

(2) A leader. The ability to give firm leadership to the congregation is the most important performing skill for a church musician. The instrumentalist is normally the conductor or song leader. In the playover or introduction, the instrumentalist must set the tempo and provide articulation and registration which inspires confidence in the congregation. Few congregations are able to transcend any lack in the skills of the instrumentalist.

As important as right notes are in the playing of hymns, the rhythm is still more important. An instrumentalist can play so fast that a congregation is left breathless or so slowly that they are left exhausted. Within these limits, the acoustics, the structure of the tune, and the content of the text should determine the phrasing. Few commas in the text call for breaks in the music.

While it is not always necessary or wise to play through the entire tune of a hymn before the congregation sings, it is necessary to play enough to allow the congregation to find the place and to establish clearly the tune and the tempo. If the tune is unfamiliar, it might be wise to play the melody line in octaves. Throughout the hymn, free use should be made of detached playing on repeated notes. If a congregation sings sluggishly, even more detached playing may be advisable. At the end of each stanza, enough time should be allowed for the congregation to take a comfortable breath. Equal time should be allowed between each stanza.

The basic tone for leading hymns is the principal chorus. Since the 8′ level is that at which the people sing, stops at pitch levels above 8′ should be added: 4′, 2 2/3′, 2′, and mixtures. Additional stops which muddy the texture are to be avoided, and the tremolo is never to be used with congregational singing. The pedals should be allowed to rest on occasional stanzas. Sufficient volume should be used so that timid singers will not fear being heard individually, but the congregation must not be overpowered. Changes in registration for various stanzas should be determined primarily by the text. The same volume and tempo should prevail through the Amen, if one is sung.

Familiar hymns can often become more interesting with judicious variations in the accompaniment. Canonic treatments, faux-bourdons, or descants can be used. On rare occasions an instrumental interlude between stanzas is effective; careful consideration should be given to the placement of such interludes within the text. The instrumentalist can work out such variations or can turn to collections of varied accompaniments such as the following:

ACCOMPANIMENTS FOR UNISON HYMN-SINGING. Compiled and edited by Gerald H. Knight, RSCM.

Bairstow, Edward C. ORGAN ACCOMPANIMENTS TO THE UNISON VERSES OF TWENTY-FOUR HYMN-TUNES FROM THE ENGLISH HYMNAL, OUP.

Bender, Jan. THE HYMN OF THE WEEK: ORGAN SETTINGS, Concordia.

FREE ACCOMPANIMENTS TO HYMNS. 4 Volumes, Augsburg.

Hancock, Gerre. ORGAN IMPROVISATION FOR HYMN-SINGING, Hinshaw Music.

HYMN PRELUDES AND FREE ACCOMPANIMENTS, Augsburg.

Johnson, David N. FREE HARMONIZATION OF TWELVE HYMN TUNES, Augsburg.

Routley, Eric. FESTIVAL PRAISE COMPANION, Hinshaw Music.

Thiman, Eric H. VARIED ACCOMPANIMENTS TO THIRTY-FOUR WELL-KNOWN HYMN TUNES, OUP.

Thiman, Eric H. VARIED HARMONIZATIONS OF FAVORITE HYMN TUNES, H. W. Gray (Belwin-Mills).

The instrumentalist uses one technique as the leader of the hymns, of "through composed" settings of canticles, and of much service music; plainsong and Anglican chant call for a different technique. Ideally, plainsong should be sung unaccompanied; certainly, however, in the learning stages and in many situations regularly thereafter, accompaniment is necessary to keep the congregation moving and on pitch. The opening intonation is usually a sufficient introduction. The organist should aim for lightness and flexibility and should use the pedals sparingly, if at all. Where available, handbells make an effective accompaniment for plainchant.

(3) An accompanist. When playing for a congregation, an instrumentalist is cast in a leadership role; when playing for a cantor, other soloist, or a choir, that of accompanist. In this role, the instrument must be subordinate to the voice. This normally calls for a more subdued registration and a willingness to allow the singer to determine the tempo.

(4) Special contributions. In addition to providing leadership for the congregation and accompaniment for the choir or cantor, the instrumentalist makes special contributions to the services. The prelude and postlude provide the musical framework for the service. Here the instrumentalist has excellent opportunities to teach new tunes to the congregation, to reinforce the themes of the liturgy of the day, and to set the mood for the people entering or leaving. A rubric in the new BOOK OF COMMON PRAYER states, "On occasion, and as appropriate, instrumental music may be substituted for a hymn or anthem" (p. 14). Often instrumental music is to be preferred to hymns or anthems at the time of the Offertory or of the Communion of the People. On occasion an instrumental fanfare might be a good substitute for the Alleluia prior to the announcement of the Gospel or for the Fraction Anthem.

Qualifications and contracts. Because the Church musician is inevitably put into the position of being a pastor and teacher, ideally this person should be well trained in the Scriptures, the liturgy, theology, and pastoral care in addition to having high competency in music. Efforts are underway to establish standards for Episcopal musicians, and there is some enthusiasm for establishing a diaconal ministry of music program. Only a fraction of the Churches are able to procure musicians with such training. High priority belongs to furthering the education of Church musicians by making it financially possible for them to attend workshops, conferences, and summer schools devoted to liturgy and Church music. Clergy should make their libraries available to musicians and guide them in their studies. In some situations it may be desirable for a portion of the compensation of the musician to be in the form of lessons under more experienced and knowledgeable Church musicians. Where this teaching is not really available or as a supplement, we recommend the use of cassettes produced by and available from Catacomb Cassettes, 3376 Peachtree Road, N.E., Atlanta, GA 30326:

- C-83 How to Sing the Liturgy
- C-113 The Holy Eucharist, Rite Two
- C-176 The Proper Prefaces from the Altar Edition of the Holy Eucharist
- C-177 Music for Ministers and Congregation
- C-232 HYMNS III (selections)
- C-245 Songs for Celebration

The musician should enter into a contract or letter of agreement with the rector. This agreement should state clearly certain things which otherwise could become sources of conflict. Where applicable, these items should appear: salary and fringe benefits; fees for weddings and funerals; time and financing for continuing education; vacation; use of the organ for practice and teaching and for pupils' practice; the availability of the choir room for the organist's use; the heating or cooling of the church and choir room; the selection of music for both the choir and the congregation; the selection of choir personnel; selection of assistants and substitutes; the relationship to the committee on liturgy; the number and nature of services with music; the number and nature of the choir(s); the number and time of rehearsals; the budget for singers, for music, and for supplementary instrumentalists; and the tuning and care of the instruments. Valuable works for clergy and musicians are:

COMPENSATION OF THE CHURCH AND SYNAGOGUE MUSICIAN. American Guild of Organists.

Farr, David. THE WORKING RELATIONSHIP BETWEEN PRINCIPAL PRIEST AND CHIEF MUSICIAN, Commission on Liturgy and Church

Music, Diocese of Los Angeles, P.O. Box 2164, Los Angeles, California 90051.

Purchasing and maintaining instruments. The pipe organ continues to be the most desirable and satisfying instrument for the leading of congregational singing, for the accompaniment of choir or cantor, and for the performance of a great portion of the instrumental music written for the Church. Where space and budget are limited, there are still available small organs adequate for the requirements of the liturgy. The organ should stand free within the room, preferably on the east-west axis; it should not be hidden and muffled in a closet or around a corner.

If a true pipe organ cannot be obtained, the next best choice in most situations is a good piano. This provides more adequate leadership than most instruments, it is easier to maintain, and competent pianists are generally easier to procure than other instrumentalists.

Throughout most of Anglican history, there were no inhibitions about using whatever instruments or instrumentalists were locally available. Harpsichord, handbells, timpani, brass (especially trumpets, trombones, or French horns), recorders, and strings (including guitars) can on occasion supplement or take the place of organ or piano. This author has in his possession an old Anglican hymnal with accompaniments for organ, harpsichord, flute or guitar.*

In many ways the least satisfactory and, in the end, the most expensive substitute for an organ or a piano is an electronic instrument. Few of these instruments, if any, provide a principal chorus, so basic and necessary for the music of the liturgy. The lifetime of these instruments is that of any normal electric appliance, whereas a real pipe organ, though more expensive initially, can be expected to last through many decades. In fact, pipe organs have been known to last through centuries, given reasonable care.

The most satisfaction and the greatest value for the dollars invested in musical instruments come with regular maintenance by a competent tuner. In many situations a long term contract is the best solution.

*THE HYMNS, ANTHEMS AND TUNES WITH THE ODE USED AT THE MAGDALEN CHAPEL, *London: Henry Thorowgood, n.d.*

Carpets, cushions, curtains, and acoustical tile are detrimental to congregational participation and other musical performance; they must be used very sparingly, if at all.

The Musical Ministry of the Clergy

Many clergy have had little opportunity to study Church music. Later, some find that the music of the Church makes greater demands upon them than they had anticipated or that the anticipated help of a knowledgeable Church musician is not available. Clergy should familiarize themselves with the new HYMNAL SUPPLEMENTS, the CHURCH HYMNAL SERIES, and THE HOLY EUCHARIST: ALTAR EDITION (providing music for many portions of various rites). They should also avail themselves of the various conferences, workshops, and summer schools in liturgy and music and of the coaching of competent local musicians. A cassette recording of the music of THE HOLY EUCHARIST: ALTAR EDITION, available from The Episcopal Radio-TV Foundation, affords potential help to many clergy. (See above, p. 40.)

The Deacon. In the Eucharistic rite, the deacon has, since the fourth century, sung the Gospel, the Prayers of the People, and the Dismissal. The Palm Sunday Procession is initiated by the deacon who also traditionally sings the Exsultet of the Great Vigil of Easter. Music for each of these appears in THE HOLY EUCHARIST: ALTAR EDITION and its supplement, PROPER LITURGIES FOR SPECIAL DAYS. Even if none of the celebrant's parts are sung, it is still fitting for the deacon to sing any or all of the deacon's portions of the rites.

The Celebrant. The Eastern Churches still maintain the old tradition of singing all of the celebrant's portion. Various factors caused the breakdown of this custom in the West in the late medieval period. Merbecke essentially attempted to revive it in the BOOKE OF COM-

MON PRAIER NOTED (1550). THE HOLY EUCHARIST: ALTAR EDITION provides music for all of the celebrant's portions of the rite except the Absolution and the Post-Sanctus of the Eucharistic Prayer. It is anticipated that musical settings of all the Eucharistic Prayers will soon become available; in the meantime, the Preface tones can be applied throughout the Prayers.

The Rector. The rector has special responsibilities for the music program, for ultimately the rector is responsible for hiring and firing, for entering into contracts or letters of agreement with church musicians. The rector, as chairman of the vestry, has some oversight of the music budget. As chairman of the liturgy committee and as chief liturgical officer of the parish, the rector is in a position to exercise a tremendous influence on the music program. When there is competent professional or volunteer leadership, the rector is wise to delegate much of this authority but is still ultimately responsible for the liturgy and music of the church. (See Canon 6, "Of the Music of the Church", p. 16, above). Some parishes have found it helpful to have a "choir warden" with seat and voice on the vestry to function as a liaison between the choir and rector and the choir and vestry.

In hiring a church musician the rector should be concerned for the pastoral instincts and abilities of the applicant, for the church musician is inevitably cast into a pastoral role. Will the musician give top priority to the hymns and service music of the people and provide for them leadership which will encourage that "full, conscious, and active participation . . . demanded by the very nature of the liturgy"* ? Is the applicant adept at teaching enthusiastically new hymns and service music to enrich, enlarge, and upgrade the liturgical repertoire of the congregation? Does this person have sufficient grasp of liturgical and theological principles to contribute to the education of the congregation and to have a voice in the planning of the rites? Can the applicant contribute to the liturgical life of the people? Given satisfaction on these counts, the rector should proceed to test other areas. Will the applicant be able to work with the choir in providing leadership for the congregation and in helping them to learn new music? Will the

* CONSTITUTION ON THE SACRED LITURGY, 14.

applicant be able to direct the choir in anthems and other music beyond the capability of the congregation? Will the applicant be able to make offerings of instrumental music?

The Musical Ministry of the Committee on Liturgy

Every parish should have a committee on liturgy. This committee should include: the clergy; the church musician; representatives of the vestry, the altar guild, the layreaders, the Christian education program, and the ushers; and other persons representative of various ages, educational backgrounds, and approaches to worship. There should not be a separate music committee.

Functions of a committee on liturgy. The primary function of the committee on liturgy is to listen to the congregation, to evaluate the rites, and to provide feedback for the clergy, musicians, layreaders, ushers, altar guild, and servers. (This should not take the place of a regular Monday morning evaluation by the clergy and musician, with videotapes of the service where possible.) Periodically the committee on liturgy should brainstorm in the search for new ideas, new approaches.

Whether the committee on liturgy should plan the principal services in detail from week to week is open to question, but it should certainly have involvement in major decisions and changes. Not only will the opinions of the group be helpful, but also this group, having been consulted, will be in a position to communicate to others the rationale for programs and/or changes.

Whether it is done by the entire committee on liturgy, by a selected group from the committee, or simply by the clergy and musician, the planning of the rites week by week should be the responsibility of more than one person. This planning should begin with a study of the lectionary for the day and should occur several weeks in advance even though certain details may have to be changed or modified later. Otherwise, music cannot be procured, and various options possible with advance thought are not feasible. Before summer vacations clergy and musician should complete planning for the fall through Christmas. Then in the fall they should finish planning for Lent and Easter. Some of the best planning for the rites of a particular day on next year's calendar occurs the morning after this year's rites. The clergy and musician should keep notebooks with plans and cautions for serious consideration in the Monday morning evaluation sessions.

A basic function of a committee on liturgy is interpretation to the congregation. Lay persons on the committee can often be much more effective than the clergy or musician.

Bibliography for a committee on liturgy. The members of the committee on liturgy should be encouraged to study the history and rationale of the liturgy. Some helpful books are:

Babin, David E. PRAISE THE LORD: A GUIDE TO THE PROPOSED PRAYER BOOK, Forward Movement.

Barrett, James E. THE HYMNARY: A TABLE FOR SERVICE PLANNING. Privately printed by the author, 1315 East 35th Street, Baltimore, MD 21218.

Borsch, Frederick H. INTRODUCING THE LESSONS OF THE CHURCH YEAR: A GUIDE FOR LAY READERS AND CONGREGATIONS, New York: Seabury Press, 1978.

Bushong, Ann Brooke. A GUIDE TO THE LECTIONARY, New York: Seabury Press, 1978.

CHRISTIAN INITIATION: A THEOLOGICAL AND PASTORAL COMMENTARY ON THE PROPOSED RITES. Associated Parishes.

ENVIRONMENT AND ART. National Bishops' Committee on the Liturgy.

HANDBOOK FOR LITURGY COMMITTEES. Liturgical Conference.

Hatchett, Marion J. COMMENTARY ON THE AMERICAN PRAYER BOOK, New York: Seabury Press, 1980.

Hatchett, Marion J. A MANUAL OF CEREMONIAL FOR THE NEW PRAYER BOOK, Sewanee: St. Luke's Journal of Theology, 1977.

Hatchett, Marion J. SANCTIFYING LIFE, TIME AND SPACE, New York: Seabury Press, 1976.

Hovda, Robert. STRONG, LOVING AND WISE: PRESIDING IN LITURGY. Liturgical Conference.

MINISTRY I: HOLY BAPTISM. Associated Parishes.

MINISTRY II: LAITY, BISHOPS, PRIESTS, AND DEACONS. Associated Parishes.

MUSIC IN CATHOLIC WORSHIP. National Bishops' Committee on the Liturgy.

PARISH EUCHARIST. Associated Parishes.

Porter, H. Boone. KEEPING THE CHURCH YEAR, New York: Seabury Press, 1978.

Price, Charles P. INTRODUCING THE PROPOSED BOOK: PRAYER BOOK STUDIES 29 REVISED, New York: The Church Hymnal Corporation.

Price, Charles P. and Weil, Louis. LITURGY FOR LIVING: THE CHURCH'S TEACHING SERIES 5, New York: Seabury Press, 1979.

Sydnor, William. THE REAL PRAYER BOOK: 1549 TO THE PRESENT, Wilton, Connecticut: Morehouse-Barlow, 1978.

THE EPISCOPAL CHOIRMASTER'S HANDBOOK. Published annually, Handbook Foundation, 524 Fourth Street, Sauk Centre, MN 56378.

THE GREAT VIGIL OF EASTER. Associated Parishes.

THE HOLY EUCHARIST: RITE TWO — A COMMENTARY. Associated Parishes.

PART TWO:

Hymns, Psalms, Service Music, Anthems, Instrumental Voluntaries

Hymns

Hymns are the "take home package" of the congregation. People's theology is almost surely more heavily influenced by the hymns which they sing than by the sermons which they hear or the prayers which they pray. This is but one illustration of the power of music and of the importance of making right choices in planning services.

Evaluating hymns. Hymns must be evaluated in terms of both text and tune and the particular wedding of text and tune.

Though hymns have the nature of poetry, they are a unique medium. Very few items from the corpus of great poetry are usable as hymnody. Because they are linked with music, hymns must be written in units suited to musical phrasing. A hymn is poor if the music makes nonsense of the text. Consider these two examples where musical lines and textual lines are at odds:

> To thee the travail deep was known
> That made the whole creation groan
> Till thou, Redeemer, shouldest free
> Thine own in glorious liberty.
>
> When the old world drew on toward night,
> Thou camest, not in splendor bright
> As monarch, but the humble child
> Of Mary, blameless mother mild.
>
> Come in thy holy might, we pray;
> Redeem us for eternal day
> From every power of darkness, when
> Thou judgest all the sons of men. (vv. 2, 3, & 5 of Hymn 6)
>
> Anoint them prophets! Make their ears attent
> To thy divinest speech; their hearts awake
> To human need; their lips make eloquent
> For righteousness that shall all evil break. (v. 2 of Hymn 220)

On the other hand, when linked with its music, such simple lyrics as those of "Were you there when they crucified my Lord?" make a great hymn.

Not all of the hymns in THE HYMNAL 1940 are suitable for use in public worship. Many of those listed in the Subject Index under "Personal Religion" (404-490) are more appropriate to private devotions than to corporate worship. In fact, some of these, because of their subjectivity, would destroy the spirit of corporate worship (for example, Hymn 438, "I need thee every hour"). Other hymns are appropriate for use in pageants but hardly in liturgical services (for example, Hymn 38, "Here betwixt ass and oxen mild"). Others are fun to sing around the piano in the parish house or in the home but are hardly suitable for use in the services of the Church (for example, 262, "Remember all the people" or 359, "Golden harps are sounding").

Other hymns are unsuited to use in the services of the Church because of questionable theology (for example, 122, "Angels and ministers, spirits of grace" because of its body-soul dualism which contradicts Christian doctrines of creation and resurrection; 535, "Rise up, O men of God!," or 536, "Turn back, O man," with their Pelagianism; 519, "Once to every man and nation," with its lines "Some great cause, God's new Messiah" and "Jesus' bleeding feet I track,/Toiling up *new* Calvaries ever").

Other hymns are not suitable because of a faulty imperialistic missionary theology (for example, 147, "God of our fathers," which speaks of "lesser breeds without the law") or because of sexism (for example, 535, "Rise up, O men of God") or because of racism (for example, 189, "And now, O Father, mindful of the love," in which we pray that our dear ones might be kept "white and clear").

Texts expressing in objective terms the praise of God or the proclamation of the Gospel or providing an appropriate corporate response to the Word or Sacrament best serve the liturgy and best teach the people.

A good hymn tune should be simple and easy for the congregation to sing. Those so simple that a congregation can pick them up on first hearing (for example, many of the "gospel songs") soon become tiresome and cloying. A hymn tune should be simple enough and yet have enough character so that, once learned, it stays with the congregation. It should be written for performance by a congregation rather than by a choir. (For examples of tunes written for choir and not usable in most congregations see Hymn 371, "Creator Spirit, by whose aid," or some of the "choir tunes" of Horatio Parker such as 390, "O 'twas a joyful sound to hear"). Whenever possible the musical accents should agree with the word accents (contrast, for example, the first tune of 126, "For all the saints," where this accordance is evident with the second tune where this agreement is lacking). A good hymn tune has distinction and beauty in the melody; it is not dependent on harmony for its main effect (note how the interest in the second tune of 172, "Now the day is over," depends upon the harmony). The harmonization should provide some melodic interest for all parts (Hymn 440, (first tune), "Watchman, tell us of the night," provides little interest in the alto part). A tune needs sufficient variety in the rhythm and melody to maintain interest through several stanzas. (How dull the second tune of 292, "Songs of praise the angels sang," with a playover and six repetitions!) The melodic range should be suitable for congregational singing. (The normal congregational range is from middle C to the second D above.) A tune with strong current associations with a secular text should be shelved for a period of time. In some congregations certain tunes must be avoided because they have strongly unpleasant associations with texts from other religious traditions. The tune should express a mood corresponding with that of the words. (Contrast the text of 58, "Weary of earth, and laden with my sin," with its happy tune; many feel that, despite the real worth and great popularity of the tune *Bohemian Brethren*, it would be even better linked with a strong hymn of praise and that its present text in THE HYMNAL 1940, "Lord Christ, when first thou cam'st to men" needs a more intense tune.) Great strength derives from a traditional association of a strong tune with an appropriate text. Many of our hymns, such as "A mighty fortress" and "O come all ye faithful," fall into this category. "O God, our help in ages past" and "Jesus Christ is risen today" are other examples.

Often a judicious selection of stanzas serves the liturgy of the day much better than the use of the whole text. This is especially true of a hymn used as a Sequence because a lengthy hymn at this point, rather than highlighting the Readings, sometimes interrupts the movement of the Liturgy of the Word. An unduly lengthy hymn at this point separates the first two Readings and the Psalm from the Gospel and sermon. When omitting stanzas, careful consideration must be given to the integrity and completeness of the remaining text.

The use of the metrical index. Clergy and church musicians should learn to use the metrical indexes in the back of THE HYMNAL 1940 (pp. 815-818) and in HYMNS III. Thoughtful use of these indexes makes possible the use of many texts which might otherwise be unusable because they appear with a tune unknown to the congregation or with a tune considered unworthy or unsuitable. (A list of suggested alternative tunes appears immediately after the introduction to HYMNAL SUPPLEMENT II.)

In the metrical index the hymns are categorized according to the number of syllables in each line. The most common metrical patterns are:

66. 86 (called Short Metre and abbreviated S.M.)
86. 86 (called Common Metre and abbreviated C.M.)
88. 88 (called Long Metre and abbreviated L.M.)
77. 77
76. 76. D. (The "D" in this and other patterns means "doubled"; it indicates that the same metrical pattern is repeated a second time.)

In theory a text in any metrical pattern could be sung to any tune of that pattern. In practice the poetic accents of some texts make them unusable with certain tunes of the same metre. For example, though the text "Come, risen Lord, and deign to be our guest" (THE HYMNAL 1940, 207; HYMNS III, H-173) and the tune *Slane* (THE HYMNAL 1940, 122) are both 10. 10. 10. 10., they will not work together for the text is iambic and the tune dactylic.

In making substitutions one must be careful to choose tunes in keeping with the texts. A strong tune sometimes redeems a weak text. As an experiment sing the text printed in THE HYMNAL 1940 at 422, "What a friend we have in Jesus," or that at 394, "Through the night of doubt and sorrow," with the tune *Ebenezer* (*Ton-y-Botel*), 519. Conversely a weak tune trivializes a strong text. Sing the text printed at

103, "See the Conqueror mounts in triumph," or that at 479, "Love divine, all loves excelling," to the tune *Erie*, 422.

For several reasons, the choice of hymns is one of the most important aspects in planning any service. Hymns are a primary element in the participation of the people and help to gather the individuals into a corporate body. Well chosen hymns provide appropriate accompaniments or responses of the people to the various elements of the rites. And often one of the hymns stays in a person's mind, forms the "take home package" and provides material for meditation and remembrance in the following days. The choice of hymns, as much as any other element, sets the tone or mood of the season. For example, there should be a radical contrast between the hymns used in Lent and those used in the Easter Season, between those used in Advent and those used at Christmas. The placement of a hymn must receive careful consideration. Not only must the text be appropriate; the tune must also be suitable. A tune good for an opening hymn, for example, would often be too big and imposing for use as a Sequence for it would tend to separate the prior Readings from the Gospel and sermon. It might also be too imposing for use at the offering for there it would overpower the Sanctus of the Eucharistic Prayer. Careful choice of hymns can contribute significantly to the solemnity, beauty, joy, and enthusiasm which the worship of God deserves.

Psalms and Canticles

Prose psalms and/or canticles are used in most of the rites of the new BOOK OF COMMON PRAYER. A Gradual is appointed for use in the Liturgy of the Word at the Eucharist and at other rites (marriage, burial, ordination, celebration of a new ministry, consecration of a church). The Gloria in excelsis or some other appropriate canticle may be used in the entrance rite of the Eucharist except in Advent or Lent. On certain occasions a canticle may take the place of the Gradual Psalm, and at times a canticle is appropriate at the entrance of the ministers, between the Epistle and Gospel, at the Offertory or during the Communion of the People. The use of psalms and of canticles is required in the Daily Offices. It is generally appropriate to sing them.

Both plainchant (plainsong) and Anglican chant settings are provided for all of the canticles of the new Prayer Book in the publication, THE BOOK OF CANTICLES: *Church Hymnal Series II*. For some canticles other settings are provided as well. Plainchant settings of the psalms appointed in the Eucharistic lectionary are provided in the publication, GRADUAL PSALMS, ALLELUIA VERSES AND TRACTS, compiled by Richard Crocker for The Standing Commission on Church Music. At the time of this writing both plainchant and Anglican chant psalters are being prepared.

Good chanting is essentially good reading on a musical tone. The rhythms and accents are essentially those of good reading. The time value of the notes is simply that of the syllables to which they are sung in Anglican chant, and for the most part, in plainchant as well. The recitation may consist of a single unaccented syllable, in which case it would be passed over lightly, or it may consist of a dozen or more syllables, in which case it would be prolonged to allow for the unhurried singing of every syllable with natural stresses.

Plainchant. A plainchant psalm tone consists of five parts:

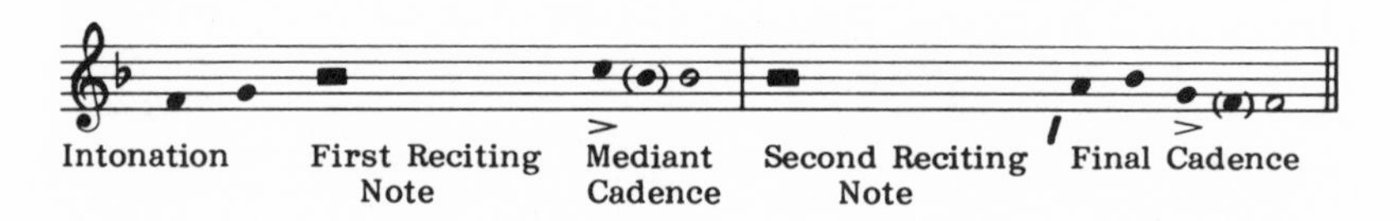

The intonation is sung to the first syllables of the first verse of any psalm or canticle. In responsorial psalms it is sung at the beginning of each verse which follows a refrain. In the Gospel canticles (Benedictus Dominus Deus, Magnificat, and Nunc dimittis) and sometimes in other canticles it is sung at the beginning of each verse.

All syllables in the first half of the verse not sung to the intonation or to the mediant cadence are sung to the first reciting note. (In rare instances the reciting note is omitted.)

The mediant cadence contains one or two accented notes to which are sung the final accented syllables of the first half of the verse. Other notes in the mediant cadence are sung to unaccented syllables or omitted. If the final syllable is accented, any note or notes which follow the final accented note of the music are omitted.

In the second half of the verse the second reciting note and the final cadence are used in the same manner in which the first reciting note and mediant cadence are used in the first half.

Whenever possible, plainsong should be unaccompanied. Simple accompaniments are provided in THE BOOK OF CANTICLES; these illustrate principles of plainsong accompaniment. Four-part harmony should be avoided as much as possible. The accompaniment should be light and flexible so that it will not hinder the supple movement of the voices. Repeated notes should normally be sustained, and 16′ tone should be used sparingly, if at all. In many instances, the intonation is a sufficient introduction, but if the tune is not well known, the whole melody should be played as an introduction. If unaccompanied, the cantor should sing the first half of the first verse and the group should then join in for the remaining portion of the verse; if accompanied, however, the whole group, accompanied, should sing the whole of the first verse after an instrumental introduction consisting of the intonation or the whole verse.

Anglican chant. Anglican chant developed from plainchant. It is an art form of great beauty when sung in four-part harmony by carefully rehearsed choirs. Many congregations sing Anglican chant with affection and enthusiasm.

An Anglican chant consists of two phrases, one of four notes in duration, followed by one of six notes. A double, triple, or quadruple chant consists of a doubling, tripling, or quadrupling of this basic pattern. Because of the fixed design of Anglican chant, a text must be pointed so that certain accented syllables will be sung to particular notes — the second and fourth notes of each section and the sixth note of the final section. The first note of each section, the reciting note, may be associated with only a single unaccented syllable (it may, in fact, on occasion be omitted) or it may be associated with a dozen or more syllables. The musical notation defines the pitch but not the duration of any note.

THE BOOK OF CANTICLES uses several marks to indicate the pointing. The short bar lines before accented syllables are equivalent to the bar lines in the music. Two dots over a syllable indicate that one syllable is extended over two notes. A staple over two (or sometimes three) syllables indicates that these are sung to the same note. A dash prior to a short bar line indicates that the reciting note is to be skipped.

The accompaniment should be light and flexible, and "imperceptibly ahead of the singing."* The singers must not have to pull the accompanist along. The pedals should be used sparingly, if at all.

Other forms of chant. Plainsong and Anglican chant form the basic musical heritage for the singing of psalms and canticles. But even as they represent the culmination of a long development, newer forms are beginning to evolve in our day. Joseph Gelineau's settings represent an imaginative, musical and singable approach. An example of this work is in THE BOOK OF CANTICLES. Other ways of chanting are also included in that work: several chants by Norman Mealy, Jack Noble White, and a setting by Ronald Arnatt.

The important thing to remember is that the singing of psalms and canticles is by no means restricted to the traditional form. Congregations may want to explore new forms, keeping in mind appropriateness in the selection and excellence in preparation.

**Carl Halter,* THE PRACTICE OF SACRED MUSIC, *St. Louis: Concordia, 1955, p. 28.*

Music for the Eucharist

The Eucharistic rite involves music in several different ways: the Gloria in excelsis, or other song of praise of the entrance rite; the Kyrie; the Trisagion; the Creed; the Sanctus and Benedictus qui venit; the Memorial Acclamation; the Lord's Prayer; and the Fraction Anthem. Certain parts may be sung by the celebrant or assisting ministers. (See HEAE.) The settings for these songs should be such that priest and people are in dialogue and that the congregation can sing them well, preferably without being bookbound.

Although composers have often provided "masses" or "services" with music for each of the common texts, it is perfectly permissible to combine elements from several different composers or services within the same rite.

The service music should be varied, at least seasonally. Most congregations should probably aim at learning at least three settings of each rite — a more somber setting for use in Advent and Lent, a more festive one for Christmas through the First Sunday after the Epiphany and for Easter through the Day of Pentecost, and another setting for more general use. Although in some congregations the use of additional settings might be desirable, there should not be so much variation that the congregation cannot participate with confidence.

Anthems

Judicious choice of anthems within the capability of the choir can contribute to the worship of the congregation in several ways. The use of new hymns as anthems is one of the most effective ways of teaching new hymns to the congregation. Anthems enhance a rite with music beyond the ability of the congregation and expose them to a great variety of music from the Church's heritage. They also allow the choir opportunity to make a special offering. Anthem preparation interests and challenges a choir and maintains the morale of a group of dedicated, able musicians. Close attention to textual meaning and its musical interpretation can provide a significant theological learning experience for them.

In the new BOOK OF COMMON PRAYER the word "anthem" refers to music sung by a choir or cantor rather than by the congregation. In the Roman rite anthems came into use about the fifth century in conjunction with the three processions — the entrance of the clergy, the Offertory procession, and the procession of the people to the Communion stations. The use of music by the choir (or a cantor) rather than music with congregational participation (except possibly through the singing of a responsorial verse) left the people free to listen, watch, and participate in the action.

In the new BOOK OF COMMON PRAYER an anthem is listed among the options for use at each of these three processions. Anthems are specified in the rubrics rather than hymns or psalms, at the Breaking of the Bread in the Eucharistic rites and at the lighting of the candles in An Order of Worship for Evening. At these times the congregation should not be bookbound but free to be involved in liturgical actions. In addition, an anthem is also an option at the place of the Gradual and of the Sequence. On occasion an anthem setting of the Psalm of the Day would be appropriate for the Gradual, and at times a brief anthem providing a response to the Epistle or an introduction to the Gospel would be appropriate in place of a Sequence or an Alleluia Verse.

On occasion, if the congregation has participated in an entrance hymn, it is acceptable to use an anthem setting of the Gloria in excelsis or of another canticle in the entrance rite of the Eucharistic rite. Anthem settings of canticles may sometimes be appropriate in the Daily Offices. The rubric after the fixed Collects of the Daily Offices allows for an anthem. This is the point at which, in classical Anglicanism, anthems have traditionally been sung.

In addition to their use in regular services, anthems are suggested in some of the Proper Liturgies for Special Days: at the beginning of the Liturgy of the Palms on Palm Sunday and after the blessing over the palms (pp. 270-271); during the washing of the feet on Maundy Thursday (pp. 274-275); and during the devotions before the cross on Good Friday (pp. 281-282). Among the pastoral Offices, in addition to the anthems which may be sung for the Eucharist, an anthem is suggested at a marriage after the Declaration of Consent (p. 425) and at the wedding party's departure from the church (p. 432). At a burial an anthem is suggested at the beginning of the rite (pp. 469 and 491-492); at the Commendation (pp. 482-483 and 499); at the bearing of the body from the church (pp. 483-484 and 500); and at the committal (pp. 484-485 and 501).

Evaluating anthems for use in liturgical services. Anthems should be suited to their use. The text of an anthem should relate to the particular service being celebrated. The tune should be in keeping with the mood of the service. The range, the balance of parts, and the degree of difficulty should be within the musical command of the choir. An anthem should be consonant with its position in the rite; it should enhance the flow of the service. Care should be exercised lest the anthem assume the climactic position rightly belonging to the Eucharistic Prayer.

A list of collections of suitable anthems appears in Chapter I (p. 33).

Hymns as choir anthems. Hymns used as choir anthems can heighten appreciation of a familiar text and/or tune and provide one of the most effective ways of teaching new hymns. Interest increases when some stanzas are sung in unison, others in harmony; some sung as solos or separately by men, women, or children; some accompanied, others a capella. Descants or faux-bourdons or varied organ accompaniments also may be used (see above, pp. 29 and 38). A brief prelude may be used as an introduction (see THE PARISH ORGANIST (Concordia) and HYMN PRELUDES AND FREE ACCOMPANIMENTS (Augsburg) for suitable brief introductions). Interludes may be used between stanzas. Sometimes the last verse may be printed in the service leaflet and the congregation asked to join in. Rather than singing the entire hymn a judicious selection of stanzas is often desirable.

Instrumental Voluntaries

This is the first edition of THE BOOK OF COMMON PRAYER which explicitly recognizes the contribution of instrumental music. Instrumental voluntaries are an effective means of teaching new music, of heightening an appreciation of familiar texts and tunes, of setting the stage for the rite, of providing opportunity for a special offering by the instrumentalists, and of exposing the congregation to a tremendous repertoire of worthy music.

Instrumental music based on hymns used in the service or on hymns or chorales thematically related to the service is normally most appropriate. The music should contribute to the rite; it should not merely entertain the congregation or exhibit the virtuosity of the instrumentalist or serve to cover worse noises.

The prelude sets the stage for the service, preparing the people to enter into the mood of the rite. It may often help the people to participate in some of the music of the rite by exposing them to it beforehand. (Note that on certain occasions a musical prelude is forbidden or undesirable [see THE BOOK OF COMMON PRAYER, pp. 142, 264, 276, 283, and 285].) The postlude sends the people on their way with a dominant theme of the service still in their minds.

In addition to the prelude and postlude, there are other opportunities for instrumental music in the rites. A rubric on page 14 states, "On occasion, and as appropriate, instrumental music may be substituted for a hymn or anthem." Instrumental music is often appropriate at the Offertory as a prelude to the Eucharistic Prayer and at the Communion of the People. On occasion it may be used appropriately as a response to a Lesson. Often it is an effective accompaniment to the entrance or exit of the ministers. Sometimes a brief selection fits in place of the Sequence or Alleluia Verse (compare p. 572) or in place of a Fraction Anthem. Instrumental music may accompany outdoor processions as is specifically suggested at the consecration of a church (p. 567).

Evaluating instrumental voluntaries. An instrumental voluntary makes a statement just as much as an anthem or a hymn and should be as carefully evaluated for its contribution to the particular service. It should be in keeping with the mood of the season and the rite. It should be suitable for the instrument(s) used and within the capability of the instrumentalist(s).

Basic collections of organ music.

Listed below are several of the most useful general collections of organ music.

FOR MANUALS ONLY. 8 short pieces, old and new, OUP.

SEASONAL CHORALE PRELUDES. Books I and II, OUP.

EASY MODERN ORGAN MUSIC FOR MANUALS. (ed. Trevor) OUP.

OLD ENGLISH ORGAN MUSIC. (ed. Trevor) 6 Books or complete in one volume, OUP.

ORGAN MUSIC FOR MANUALS. (ed. Trevor) 6 Books, OUP.

TEN 18TH CENTURY ENGLISH VOLUNTARIES. (ed. R. Peek) Concordia.

MANUALS ONLY. (ed. E. Power Biggs) Associated Music.

ITALIAN ORGAN MUSIC OF THE 18TH CENTURY. (ed. Milton Sutter) Harold Flammer.

BAROQUE MUSIC FOR MANUALS. (ed. S. Drummond Wolf) Volume I & II, Concordia.

THE ORGANIST'S COMPANION. (ed. Wayne Leupold) a bi-monthly journal of easy organ music, mostly manuals alone, McAfee Music.

TALLIS TO WESLEY SERIES. Various Eng. composers, Hinrichsen (Peters).

THE ANGLO-AMERICAN BOOK OF 18TH CENTURY ORGAN MUSIC. (ed. Joanne S. Hart) The Sacred Music Press.

LIBER ORGANI SERIES. Schott.

THE PARISH ORGANIST SERIES. Concordia.

EARLY ORGAN MUSIC SERIES. Novello. (Various works).

SPIELBUCH FÜR DIE KLEINORGEL. Books I & II, Peters.

A LITTLE KEYBOARD BOOK. (ed. J. S. Darling) Colonial Williamsburg, Inc.

Silva Iberica. Books I & II, (ed. Kastner) Schott.

Early Tudor Organ Music. Vol. I & II, Stainer & Bell.

Buxheimer Orgelbuch. Vol. I & II, Hinrichsen (Peters).

80 Chorale Preludes. (ed. Hermann Keller) German Masters of the 17th and 18th centuries, Peters.

Collections of works of individual composers of particular use include the following:

J.S. Bach. Orgelbüchlein.

Johannes Brahms. Eleven Chorale Preludes, Mercury Music (Theodore Presser).

Dietrich Buxtehude. Chorale Preludes, Peters.

Johann Pachelbel. Chorale Preludes, Kalmus.
Partitas, Kalmus.
Fugues on the Magnificat, Novello.

Flor Peeters. Chorale Preludes, Peters. (Various collections).

Samuel Scheidt. Das Görlitzer Tabulaturbuch, Peters.

Ralph Vaughan Williams. Three Preludes Founded on Welsh Hymn Tunes, Stainer & Bell.

Louis Vierne. 24 Pieces in Free Style, Durand.

Healey Willan. Five Preludes on Plainchant Melodies, Oxford.
Six Chorale Preludes (2 sets), Concordia.
Ten Chorale Preludes (3 sets), Peters.
36 Short Preludes and Postludes on well-known Hymn Tunes, Peters.

Alec Wyton. Preludes for Genesis, Agape.

Various liturgical versets from suites and masses by French composers of the 17th and 18th centuries, especially works by Couperin, Du Mage, Clerambault, and Guilain are especially usable as organ voluntaries.

PART THREE:

Educating and Inspiring the People

Music in Christian Education

Christian education implies that learning is going on for the entire congregation in various ways and through various structures. It is a very complex operation and varies from church to church. Imaginative opportunities must be created to talk about, present, practice, experience and participate in liturgy and its music.

These opportunities would help children to learn hymns and service music. Adults should have seminars on liturgy and its meaning. There should also be open rehearsals for congregations at various times — before service, during the service, at a separate time. Choirs can give demonstrations as a means of showing and teaching the congregation. A hymn sing with some old favorites along with new hymns is another possibility. On occasion a hymn sing designed as a homily might be appropriate. Classes in church school can learn hymns for the current Church season. These hymns must be those for the liturgy, not the "easy" hymns which underestimate children's ability to appreciate, learn and use the best in church music.

Congregations can no longer rely on a limited number of hymns for full participation in the service. They must develop a greater musical knowledge to facilitate participation in new hymns and service music.

Teaching New Hymns and Service Music

The learning and singing of new hymns is important to the spiritual development of individuals and of congregations. An increased repertoire opens additional possibilities for relating hymnody to the lectionary. Hymn singing then becomes an integral part of the liturgy. Often new, stronger tunes bring out the hidden worth of familiar texts. For example, compare the seriousness and intensity of the first tune with the lack of such in the second tune of Hymn 416 in THE HYMNAL 1940, "O for a closer walk with God." In a similar vein, compare the first and second tunes of 479, "Love divine, all loves excelling."

One need not fear introducing new hymns because experience indicates that many congregations can maintain a repertoire of two to three hundred hymn tunes. If the repertoire is stretched too far beyond this, many tunes are not used with enough frequency for the congregation to feel at ease with them. If judicious use is made of the metrical index (see above, pp. 52-53), this number of tunes makes available an overwhelming majority of the texts of the THE HYMNAL 1940 and of HYMNS III.

New hymns should be carefully chosen for their usefulness. When it is desirable to replace a familiar tune with a superior new tune, we recommend the following procedure: for example, if the congregation is familiar with the second tune, *Sawley*, of Hymn 462, "Jesus, the very thought of thee," and one wishes to switch to the unfamiliar first tune, *Windsor*, it might be wise to omit the use of this text for a period of time. During that time the tune *Windsor* might be taught and used with the text "My God, how wonderful thou art" (284). After this tune has been well learned, the text "Jesus, the very thought of thee" may then be sung to it.

In introducing a new hymn, the choir should sing the melody in unison, or for the sake of absolute clarity in certain hymns, it may be desirable to have the hymn melody sung by a soloist or a cantor. The organist might play only the melody in a play-through of a new hymn. A piano might be preferable to an organ for strong, rhythmic leadership in teaching new hymns.

Much can be gained by introducing new hymns and service music in some way before expecting congregational involvement. Some churches use a "Hymn of the Month" plan in which the choir or cantor first perform it. Relevant remarks about its history and use are presented on one Sunday. The hymn is then used as a congregational hymn on the remaining Sundays of the month. However, great attention should be given to its liturgical suitability for succeeding Sundays.

Some congregations have had success with a regular monthly hymn and service practice. Others have an open choir practice once a month. Church suppers, the church school, and other informal settings provide an excellent opportunity for teaching new hymns. The more relaxed atmosphere of the parish house is often more conducive to effective teaching.

Sometimes a brief pre-service warmup is desirable. This should be exceedingly well planned to make the most economical use of time. It should probably not be aimed at producing a polished performance but only at enabling the congregation to sing with some confidence one or two of the items. If lengthier pre-service practices are desired, they should probably be announced in advance and so scheduled that the service itself can begin at the usual time.

To promote interest in new hymns, notes about hymns and stories about the circumstances of their being written can be printed in the bulletin or used in sermons. THE HYMNAL 1940 COMPANION (New York: The Church Hymnal Corporation) is a good source for such information.

People should be encouraged to possess their own copies of THE HYMNAL 1940, HYMNS III, and THE HYMNAL 1940 COMPANION. Hymns are very useful for private and family devotions. Next to the Bible and THE BOOK OF COMMON PRAYER, THE HYMNAL 1940 is the greatest source of devotional material readily available to most people. Furthermore, people whose devotional life has been nurtured on the hymnal are more receptive to learning new hymns.

A dynamic, positive, and enthusiastic attitude from the clergy, choir, and organist can make all the difference in the acceptance of new music. A choir concerned with its educational function should not be too proud to make use of hymns in place of anthems when appropriate. Interest and variation are achieved by the use of different groupings, variation between unison singing and full harmony, and the use of descants, faux-bourdons, and varied harmonizations. HYMNS III contains the last three items for a number of tunes. Some of the harmonizations provided in HYMNS III could be alternated with the harmonizations of THE HYMNAL 1940. An interesting anthem could be constructed from H-245. The first verse could be sung in unison with the accompaniment printed at H-245a, the second with the harmonization at H-245b, and the third in canon as suggested at H-245a.

Unfamiliar hymns or service music scheduled for congregational use can be used by the organist as preludes, as postludes, and as offertory or communion voluntaries. Variations can be achieved on some of the repetitions by highlighting the melody on a solo stop and by the use of varied harmonizations. (See above, p. 38). Suitable and useful preludes are available on at least half of the tunes in THE HYMNAL 1940 and HYMNS III. (See the list of hymn preludes in THE HYMNAL 1940 COMPANION.) Using a number of tunes in these ways lessens the congregation's uneasiness about singing them, for frequent hearing of a new tune will lend some feeling of familiarity.

Unless the text is appropriate only for an opening or closing hymn, it is best to use a new hymn within the service. If an unfamiliar hymn used at the beginning of a service does not elicit good congregational participation, a negative reaction, difficult or impossible to counteract, may ensue. If the final hymn is unfamiliar, no matter how many familiar tunes appeared within the service, the clergy are often met at the door with, "Why do we never sing anything familiar?"

Teaching a Different Pointing for Canticles

Several steps are advisable in teaching new pointing for canticles. If there is a choir, it should be thoroughly at home with the new pointing before exposing the congregation to it. An effective approach to teaching the choir is to have them read the words of the canticle together, verse by verse, repeating until it conveys meaning, with proper stress on the words. They should then monotone the words, in the same rhythm with the same stresses. They should then sing the canticle, maintaining this same care for the text. In many situations it would be wise for the choir to sing the canticle as an anthem, possibly two or three times, before asking the congregation to participate. For the sake of absolute clarity, it would be better for a cantor rather than the choir to model the new pointing for the congregation. Then the congregation should be alerted to the difference in pointing, followed by the same procedures used with the choir — first reading, then monotoning, last of all singing the canticle.

In teaching a new canticle, it is generally best not to use a new tune with a new text or pointing, but rather to use a tune familiar to the congregation. When teaching a new pointing for a familiar text, however, a tune associated with the old pointing should not be used. If, for example, the most familiar tunes are those by Goodson (609) for the Venite and by Russell (645) for the Jubilate, it would be good to reverse the settings.

Use of Service Leaflets

Service leaflets are a basic and essential educational tool. They help the people to find their way in the service and indicate the shape of the rite. Sometimes they may specify the theme of the service. Leaflets may either provide texts and tunes needed by the congregation or indicate clearly the books within which these texts and tunes are to be found. They should usually provide translations for any texts sung in foreign languages.

Information in the leaflet should assist the people in moving with ease through the service. Unfortunately, service leaflets sometimes provide more detail than the congregation needs, thus becoming more confusing than helpful. Congregations do not need to follow the whole text of a rite. Brief responses and refrains are often more effectively dealt with by reproduction in the service leaflet instead of a page reference. The refrains from GRADUAL PSALMS, ALLELUIA VERSES AND TRACTS and any items from MUSIC FOR MINISTERS AND CONGREGATION may be reproduced in the service leaflet without infringement of copyright. An increasing number of commercial publishers are giving permission to reproduce in a service leaflet the refrains or melody lines of hymns, psalms, canticles and service music. One should be sure to ascertain this freedom by checking the copyright permission statement in the source publication.

Reproduced below is a service leaflet prepared for a congregation still in the process of learning several of the regular responses from MUSIC FOR MINSTERS AND CONGREGATION.

Second Sunday of Easter

Organ: Prelude on *Llanfair* — Hermann Schroeder

Hymn H-130, "Christians, haste your vows to pay" — *Llanfair*

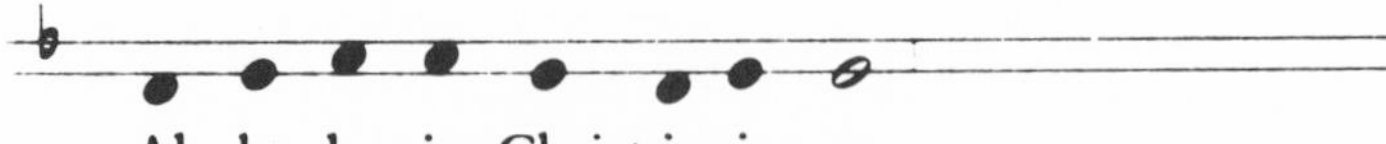

Song of Praise: C-43, "Christ our Passover" (BCP, p. 83)

The Collect of the Day

The Word of God

First Reading: *Acts 3:12a, 13-15, 17-26*

Silence

Gradual: *Psalm 111* (BCP, p. 754)

REFRAIN

Second Reading: *1 John 5:1-6*

Silence

Alleluia Verse: *John 20:29*

The Holy Gospel: *John 20:19-31*

The Sermon

The Nicene Creed (BCP, p. 358)

The Prayers of the People: Form V (BCP, p. 389)

Responses:

The Peace

The Holy Communion

Hymn 99 (stanzas 1, 4-8), "O sons and daughters, let us sing"
O filii et filiae

Eucharistic Prayer D (BCP, p. 372)

Sanctus: *Church Hymnal Series I*, p. 7 Robert J. Powell

Memorial Acclamation: *Congregational Music for Eucharist*, E-61
Robert J. Powell

The Lord's Prayer: *Congregational Music for Eucharist*, E-64
Robert J. Powell

The Breaking of the Bread

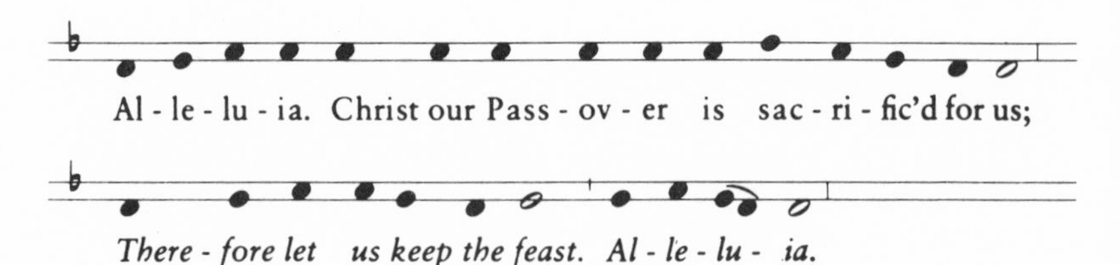

The Communion

Anthem: "This joyful Eastertide" (for text, see H-139) Dutch carol

The postcommunion prayer (BCP, p. 365)

Hymn 98, "That Easter Day with joy was bright" *Puer nobis*

The Dismissal

Organ: "*O sons and daughters, let us sing*" Jean Francois Dandrieu

PART FOUR:

Planning Music for the Rites of the Prayer Book

Principles for Choosing Hymns, Service Music, Anthems, and Instrumental Voluntaries

The music used in the services of the Church should be selected according to definite principles. To fall back on the constant use of the "old," familiar," and "well-liked" hymns, service music, anthems, and instrumental voluntaries is hardly a worthy principle. Hopefully, in the end, the new music, with frequent repetition, will become the people's own, but they cannot be expected to like every musical work on first hearing. It is important to maintain in services a balance between familiar music and that in the process of being learned.

Hymns

The hymns for a service should be chosen according to one of four principles:

(1) The thematic or liturgical principle. The choice of hymn is based on the relationship of its text to the lections, theme of the day, and the particular place it will occupy in the rite.

(2) The seasonal principle. At points in the rite for which there is no peculiarly appropriate hymn, it is suitable to use a seasonal hymn.

(3) The teaching principle. Hymns which the congregation is currently learning should be used frequently at services whenever the text is suitable.

(4) The "use in course" principle. Much of the lectionary is based on the use of psalms and lessons "in course" (that is, read sequentially). This is an assurance that fitting passages will not be overlooked in a given period of time. When hymns cannot be chosen according to the above principles, the gaps within a service should be filled according to the "use in course" principle. A definite record should be kept of the use of each hymn at the principal services.

Service Music

Analogous principles apply to the choice of service music. Each congregation should know more than one setting for each of the songs of the people. This makes possible some contrast between ordinary Sundays and the preparatory seasons of Advent and Lent, on the one hand, or the festal seasons of Christmas-Epiphany and Easter-Pentecost on the other. Settings currently being taught should be used almost exclusively for a period of time. This will quickly bring a sense of ease on the part of the congregation. A word of caution: in the emphasis on learning the new, do not neglect the use of the familiar for such an extended period of time that the people lose confidence in singing it.

Anthems

Ideally the anthem should enhance the proclamation of the lections for the day or occasion or provide a meditation on them or appropriate response to them. The text of an anthem should be suited to the action it accompanies (entrance, Offertory, or Communion). When peculiarly apt texts are not available, an anthem generally suited to the season is acceptable. When choosing music for the choir, hymns and service music projected for later congregational use should be high on the list of priorities. Finally, good anthems should not fall into disuse but should be used according to a "use in course" scheme. A definite record should be kept of the use of each anthem at a principal service.

Instrumental Voluntaries

Much the same principles as those for anthems apply to the choice of instrumental voluntaries. Those with word associations for the people, thus helping to set the stage for the particular lections, should have high priority. The voluntary should be used frequently to familiarize the people with new hymns or service music. At other times, it is fitting to employ music with no particular word associations but with content which helps to set the stage for a particular service or expresses an appropriate musical response to the rite.

Planning Music for The Daily Office

Two strands of tradition lie behind the Daily Office of THE BOOK OF COMMON PRAYER: the weekday forms of the Liturgy of the Word, centered in the reading and exposition of the Scriptures, and the periods of private prayer which later within monasticism developed into corporate Offices which sanctify with prayer the principal divisions of the day. Because of the nature of the Daily Office, permission to precede or follow an Office with a hymn has been withdrawn. A hymn seems inappropriate before the Opening Preces of Morning Prayer. Note that Morning or Evening Prayer may be used as the Liturgy of the Word at the Eucharist in conformity with directions on pages 142 and 322, or 354.

Daily Morning Prayer

Pre-service music. Congregational participation can be greatly enhanced if the time immediately before the Office is devoted to familiarizing the people with the music. The music of the Office itself may be used or preludes based on it. In addition to music used for teaching purposes, other instrumental music is often excellent at this point.

Opening sentences. If used, the opening sentence(s) may be monotoned.

Opening Preces. For the music of the Opening Preces, see THE BOOK OF CANTICLES (1A, 2A, 25A, 26A).

Invitatory Psalm. Antiphons are provided for every day of the year for use with the Invitatory Psalm (BC, C-3, 6, 15, 28, 30, 36). Traditionally this Psalm is sung responsorially. The cantor or choir begins by singing the Antiphon, then repeated by the people. The choir or cantor then sings the verses with the congregation singing the Antiphon after each division of the Venite or each verse of the Jubilate. When Anglican pointing is used for the Antiphon, however, it is sung only before and after the Invitatory Psalm. The Antiphon's purpose is to highlight the emphasis of the day or season. On occasion, the congregation may sing the Invitatory Psalm, with or without the Antiphon. A metrical version of the Invitatory Psalm may also be used. (See THE HYMNAL 1940, 278 and 300 and HYMNS III, H-231 for metrical versions of Jubilate and HYMNS III, H-197 and H-243 for metrical versions of Venite.)

278	All people that on earth do dwell
300	Before the Lord Jehovah's throne
H-231	Sing, all creation
H-197	Come, sound his praise abroad
H-243	To God with gladness sing

Psalm 95 is used in its entirety on Ash Wednesday, Holy Saturday, and all Fridays during Lent. (See BCP, pp. 950-957.) It may be used at other times. For settings of this psalm see THE BOOK OF CANTICLES: C-5, 11 — 14, 29, 31 — 34.

Pascha nostrum is sung in Easter Week in place of the Invitatory Psalm and may be used until the Day of Pentecost. (See BC, C-21 to 24, 43 to 46.) An Antiphon is not used with Pascha nostrum.

Variable psalm(s). The variable psalms may be sung in unison, antiphonally, or responsorially. The antiphonal method is traditional; because of the length of selections for the Daily Office, this method seems best in most situations. Plainchant and Anglican chant are the usual setting of the psalms in the Daily Office. Plainchant is generally easier and more effective. Anglican chant is a desirable alternative with a group which sings together daily and can do parts with ease.

Gloria Patri is to be used after the last psalm and may be used after each psalm or after each section of Psalm 119. Even if the psalm is antiphonal, the Gloria Patri is sung by all. If the psalm is said, so is the Gloria Patri.

Old Testament Lesson. If the Old Testament Lesson is sung, the announcement and conclusion should also be sung. See HEAE or MMC for instructions on the singing of lessons.

Silence. A period of silence may follow the reading.

Canticle. After an Old Testament Lesson, a pre-incarnational canticle (1, 2, 4, or 8 — 14, 16) is appropriate. (See BC for plainchant, Anglican, and "through composed" settings.) The Canticle of Moses (8) is particularly appropriate in the Easter Season, and a Song of Penitence (14) during Lent or on penitential occasions. A table suggests canticles appropriate to each of the days of the week (BCP, pp. 144-145). Gloria Patri is not required but may be used after Canticles 4, 8, 9, 10, 11, or 16. (It is probably best to omit Gloria Patri if using a canticle setting with a translation different from that of THE BOOK OF COMMON PRAYER.) Canticle texts within Rite One may be used in Rite Two, and vice versa. Other previously authorized translations may be used if the music requires it. Metrical versions of the canticles may be used. (See HYMNS III, H-221, "O all ye works of God now come," for a metrical version of Benedicite, omnia opera Domini and H-193, "Blest be the God of Israel," for a metrical version of Benedictus Dominus Deus.) "In special circumstances, in place of a Canticle, a hymn may be sung" (BCP, p. 142). Services with a congregation unable to sing canticles or made up largely of children may use a hymn in place of the canticle. This could also apply to certain festal days.

New Testament Lesson. If the New Testament Lesson is sung, the announcement and conclusion should also be sung. See HEAE or MMC for instructions on singing the lessons.

Silence. A period of silence may be kept after the reading.

Sermon. If two Lessons are used, the sermon will follow at this point. (See BCP, pp. 113, 142 .)

Canticle. After a lesson from the New Testament, a post-incarnational canticle (3, 5 — 7, or 15, 17 — 21) is appropriate. (See BC for plainchant, Anglican, and "through composed" settings.) A table suggests canticles appropriate to each of the days of the week (BCP, pp. 144-145). It is traditional to omit either Gloria in excelsis or Te Deum laudamus on ordinary days of Advent or Lent. Gloria Patri is not required but may be used after canticles 3, 5, 15, 17, 19. Texts appearing in Rite Two may be used in Rite One, and vice versa. Other previously authorized translations may be used if the music requires it. Metrical versions of the canticles may be used. (See THE HYMNAL 1940, 260 for a metrical setting of Magna et mirabilia and 273 for Te Deum laudamus; see HYMNS III, H-235 for Magnificat, H-215 for

Nunc dimittis, H-195 for Dignus es, H-190 for Gloria in excelsis, and H-222 for Te Deum laudamus.)

260	How wondrous and great
273	Holy God, we praise thy Name
H-235	Tell out, my soul
H-215	Lord, let your servant go in peace
H-195	Come, let us join our cheerful songs
H-190	All glory be to God on high
H-222	O God, we praise thee

In special circumstances a hymn may be used in place of a canticle. (See above under *Canticle*.)

Gospel. If all three Lessons are used, the Gospel comes after the canticle following the New Testament reading. If it is sung, the announcement and conclusion should also be sung. See HEAE or MMC for the singing of lessons.

There is no permission to sing a hymn between the Lesson and the sermon. Nothing should intervene between the people's response to the lection and the initial sentence of the sermon. If fewer than three Lessons are used, the sermon will follow the last Lesson and precede a canticle. (See BCP, pp. 113, 142.)

Apostles' Creed. If this is monotoned, it is not good form for an organist to accompany it. Music may intrude as well as enhance. This is an occasion on which it intrudes.

Suffrages. See BC, C-1C—E; 2C—E; 25C—E; 26C—E. The responses should not be accompanied after the congregation has learned them. The second set of suffrages has been associated traditionally with the Te Deum laudamus and the Gloria in excelsis.

Collects. One or more Collects and a Prayer for mission are required except in special circumstances. See HEAE or MMC for tones for the Collects.

Hymn or anthem. Much of the English cathedral anthem repertoire was composed for use at this point in the Daily Office. This is also a good time for an Office hymn or one related to the lections of the day, a seasonal hymn or a general hymn of praise.

See page 830 of THE HYMNAL 1940 for a list of Office hymns included in that book. HYMNS III includes two translations of a traditional Office hymn for Ascension.

H-142 Christ, above all glory seated
H-143, 144 O Lord, most high, eternal King

An offering may be quietly received and placed upon the altar during the course of the hymn or anthem. Processions of a triumphal nature and presentation sentences are inappropriate in the Daily Office.

Intercessions and thanksgivings. Prayers following the Collect structure may be sung to a collect tone. Other prayers may be monotoned.

Benedicamus. For music see BC, C-1G, 2G, 25G, 26G.

The Grace. This sentence of scripture may be monotoned.

Postlude. The postlude reflects or sums up the rite. This might be the occasion to use a voluntary based on that text which best sums up the rite or one introducing an unfamiliar tune.

An Order of Service for Noonday

Prelude. See Morning Prayer (above).

Opening Preces. For the music for the Opening Preces see MNOC or BC, C-25B, 26B (Evening Prayer)

Hymn. See THE HYMNAL 1940 for traditional Office hymns for the Little Offices:

160 Come, Holy Ghost, with God the Son (for Terce, 9 a.m.)
161 O God of truth, O Lord of might (for Sext, 12 noon)
162 O God, creation's secret force (for None, 3 p.m.)

Psalm(s). For music see MNOC. The Psalm(s) may be sung as at Morning Prayer, although unison singing may be desirable because of the shorter selections. Everyone sings Gloria Patri at the end of the Psalms. If the Psalm is said, Gloria Patri must be said.

Scripture. See MNOC. The Lesson may be monotoned and the response sung.

Prayers. See MNOC. For tones for the Collects, see HEAE or MMC.

Dismissal. For the music see MNOC or BC, C-25G, 26G.

Postlude. See Morning Prayer (above).

An Order of Worship for the Evening

This Order may be used as a complete rite; as an introduction to Evening Prayer, the Holy Eucharist, or some other rite; or as the prelude to an evening meal or other activity.

"A musical prelude or processional is not appropriate" (BCP, p. 142).

Opening Acclamation. For the music see BC, C-27A — D; HEAE or MMC.

Short Lesson of Scripture. It is appropriate to sing this short Lesson according to the tone provided in HEAE, page 206, or MMC, page 34, or to monotone it.

Prayer for Light. See HEAE or MMC for collect tones.

Anthem, psalm, or silence. For traditional lucernaria texts see BOS. A cantor or choir might sing one of the traditional evening psalms (8, 23, 36, 84, 93, 113, 114, 117, 121, 134, 139, 141, 143). It is not appropriate to have a congregational hymn or psalm at this point for the attention of the people should be on the lighting of the candles rather than on a book or service sheets.

Phos hilaron. For settings of this canticle see BC, C-47 — 52. For metrical settings see:

173, 768	O Brightness of the immortal Father's face
176	O gladsome light, O grace
H-162, 163	O gracious Light, Lord Jesus Christ

The service may continue with Evening Prayer (beginning with the Psalms), with the Holy Eucharist (beginning with the Salutation and Collect of the Day), or with some other Office or devotion. If a meal or some other activity is to follow, the service may conclude with the Lord's Prayer and a Grace or Blessing or it may continue with the elements outlined on page 113 of THE BOOK OF COMMON PRAYER.

Psalm(s). These may be sung as at Morning Prayer (above).

Silence. A period of silence may follow the Psalm(s).

Collect. A Collect related to the Psalm(s) may be used. It is hoped that use of traditional psalter Collects will be revived. For collect tones see HEAE or MMC.

Lesson. The reading, with its announcement and conclusion, may be sung. A sermon, a reading, or silence may follow the Lesson.

Canticle or hymn of praise. The Magnificat, a canticle including the theme of light (for example, Surge, illuminare, Benedictus Dominus Deus, or Nunc dimittis), a hymn based on the theme of light, or a general hymn of praise may be used.

Prayers. A litany or other devotions may be sung or said.

Lord's Prayer. Even if other prayers have been said, the Lord's Prayer may be sung. It may be monotoned as in conjunction with suffrages at Morning or Evening Prayer, or a setting such as those in THE HYMNAL 1940, 705 and 722, CHURCH HYMNAL SERIES I, pages 17, 31, and 40, CME, or MMC may be used.

Concluding Collect. See HEAE or MMC for collect tones.

Blessing and Dismissal. See BC, C-27 E — H or HEAE, pages 233-235, or MMC, pages 25-27. "Alleluia, alleluia" is added to the Dismissal and response during the Easter Season.

Postlude. See Morning Prayer (above).

Daily Evening Prayer

The structure of the rite and the ceremonial action are basically the same as those for Morning Prayer (above). For music for Opening Preces see BC, C-1B, 2B, 25B, 26B. An Invitatory Psalm is not required as at Morning Prayer, but one may be used or the Phos hilaron or another hymn. (See BC, C-47 — 52 for settings of the Phos hilaron; see THE HYMNAL 1940, 173, 176, and 768; HYMNS III, H-162, 163 for metrical settings.)

173, 768	O Brightness of the immortal Father's face
176	O gladsome Light, O grace
H-162, 163	O gracious Light, Lord Jesus Christ

Normally only one Lesson would be used; the Gospel in Year One and the Epistle in Year Two. Any of the canticles of Morning Prayer may be used at Evening Prayer. In Anglicanism the Magnificat and Nunc dimittis have been traditionally associated with this Office. For music for the Suffrages see BC, C-1C, D, F; 2C, D, F; 25C, D, F; 26C, D, F.

An Order for Compline

Prelude. See Morning Prayer (above).

Preces. See MNOC or BC, C-25B (Evening Prayer) for music for Preces.

Psalm(s). See MNOC. The Psalm(s) may be sung as at Morning Prayer. Because the selections are shorter, unison singing may be desirable. All sing Gloria Patri at the end of the Psalms. If the Psalm is said, so is the Gloria Patri.

Scripture. See MNOC. The Lesson may be monotoned, and the response sung.

Hymn. An evening hymn is suitable here. Sometimes it is permissible to substitute a seasonal hymn.

Suffrages and Lord's Prayer. See MNOC.

Collects. For collect tones see HEAE or MMC.

Antiphon, Alleluias, and Nunc dimittis. See MNOC. Also see BC for other settings of Nunc dimittis.

Benedicamus and Blessing. For music see MNOC or BC, C-25G, 26G.

Postlude. If used at the end of Compline, it should be quiet and restrained.

Planning Music for the Great Litany

The Great Litany may be sung or read by the officiant, kneeling or standing in some prominent place so as to be both seen and heard.

The Great Litany may be used as an entrance rite for the Holy Eucharist. This is a dramatic way of marking the First Sunday of Advent, the First Sunday in Lent, and/or the Rogation Days.

In some architectural situations, it is possible and sometimes desirable to sing the Litany in procession either within or outside the church building. The ministers and choir or the whole congregation may participate in the procession. Where appropriate, the invocations might be sung before the altar. The procession might circle the church, then return to the altar or the chancel steps for the Lord's Prayer and the concluding collect.

For music for the Great Litany see MMC II.

Planning Music for the Church Year

Advent Season

The emphasis for the First Sunday of Advent is eschatological; for the next two Sundays the emphasis shifts to John the Baptist, and for the Last Sunday to the Annunciation. Appropriate hymns for the First Sunday include:

3 Wake, awake, for night is flying
4 Rejoice, rejoice, believers
5 Lo! he comes, with clouds descending
8 O Word, that goest forth on high
312 The Lord will come and not be slow
518 Judge eternal, throned in splendor
521 O God of earth and altar
761 Rejoice, rejoice, believers

H-104 Jesus came—the heavens adoring
H-106 O Savior, open heaven wide
H-107 Once he came in blessing
H-108 Prepare the way, O Zion
H-239 The Lord will come and not be slow

For the Second and Third Sundays:

3 Wake, awake, for night is flying
4 Rejoice, rejoice, believers
9 Hark! a thrilling voice is sounding
10 On Jordan's bank the Baptist's cry
761 Rejoice, rejoice, believers
H-103 Comfort, comfort ye my people
H-193 Blest be the God of Israel

For the Fourth Sunday:

1 Come, thou long-expected Jesus
2 O come, O come, Emmanuel
6 Creator of the stars of night
7 Hark! the glad sound! the Saviour comes
11 The King shall come when morning dawns
117 Sing of Mary, pure and lowly
118 Praise we the Lord this day
H-105 Lift up your heads, ye mighty gates
H-106 O Savior, open heaven wide
H-108 Prepare the way, O Zion
H-155 The angel Gabriel from heaven came
H-156, 157 The Christ whom earth and sea and sky
H-235 Tell out, my soul

Advent might be set apart from the Sundays after Pentecost preceding it and from the festal Christmas Season following it by beginning the Eucharistic rite with the Great Litany, possibly in procession, or with the Penitential Order.

THE BOOK OF OCCASIONAL SERVICES provides an order for an Advent Festival of Lessons and Music.

Christmas Season

Both THE HYMNAL 1940 and HYMNS III contain large sections of hymns specific to Christmas (see THE HYMNAL 1940, 12—45; HYMNS III, H-109—114.) In addition several hymns in the general sections are appropriate.

775 Joy to the world
H-190 All glory be to God on high
H-203 Glorious the day when Christ was born
H-246 Where is this stupendous stranger

THE BOOK OF OCCASIONAL SERVICES provides a vigil for use prior to the first Eucharist of Christmas, a station at a Christmas creche, and a Christmas Festival of Lessons and Music.

At some point within the Christmas Season, either on New Year's Eve, or on a Sunday after Christmas, it is appropriate to mark the New Year. This may be the Service for New Year's Eve (BOS) or, on the other hand, a simple inclusion of appropriate petitions and hymns within the rites of the First or Second Sunday after Christmas or the Feast of the Holy Name. Suitable hymns are:

276 Now thank we all our God
289 O God, our help in ages past
303 We come unto our fathers' God
425 Jesus, lead the way
434 Guide me, O thou great Jehovah
497 O God of Bethel, by whose hand
524 God of grace and God of glory
783 God of grace and God of glory
H-115 Great God, we sing that mighty hand
H-188 All my hope on God is founded
H-205 Guide me, O thou great Jehovah
H-211 If thou but suffer God to guide thee

January 1 is the Feast of the Holy Name. This day takes precedence over the Sunday. Suitable hymns include:

6 Creator of the stars of night (stanzas 1-4)
113 The ancient law departs

323 Jesus! Name of wondrous love
324 Conquering kings their titles take
325 O for a thousand tongues to sing
326 To the Name of our salvation
342 Jesus, Name all names above
355 All hail the power of Jesus' Name
356 At the Name of Jesus
366 All praise to thee, for thou, O King divine
776 O for a thousand tongues to sing
778 Jesus, Name all names above

When there is a Second Sunday after Christmas, one of three Gospels may be read: the flight into Egypt and return to Nazareth; the visit to the temple at the age of twelve; or the visit of the magi. If the emphasis is on the Holy Family and family life, related Christmas hymns or hymns with family themes may be used, such as:

276 Now thank we all our God
296 For the beauty of the earth
303 We come unto our fathers' God
504 Our Father, by whose Name
H-181 O Father blest, we ask of you

If the Gospel is the story of the visit of the magi, suitable hymns include:

28 Angels, from the realms of glory
30 The first Nowell the angel did say
36 What child is this, who, laid to rest
46 Brightest and best of the sons of the morning
47 What star is this, with beams so bright
48 Earth has many a noble city
52 As with gladness men of old
762 Brightest and best of the sons of the morning
H-116, 117 When Christ's appearing was made known (vv. 1, 2, 5)

Epiphany Season

On the feast of the Epiphany itself, when the Gospel is the story of the visit of the magi, suitable hymns include:

46 Brightest and best of the sons of the morning
47 What star is this, with beams so bright
48 Earth has many a noble city
49 From the eastern mountains
51 We three kings of Orient are
52 As with gladness men of old
762 Brightest and best of the sons of the morning
H-116, 117 When Christ's appearing was made known

For the First Sunday after the Epiphany, the Baptism of our Lord, THE BOOK OF OCCASIONAL SERVICES provides a vigil for use in connection with baptism and the Eucharist. THE HYMNAL 1940 has only three hymns mentioning the Baptism:

53 Songs of thankfulness and praise
268 I bind unto myself today
344, 779 O love, how deep, how broad, how high

For other hymns for this day see:

H-118 The sinless one to Jordan came
H-119 When Jesus went to Jordan's stream
H-120 Christ, when for us you were baptized
H-116, 117 When Christ's appearing was made known (vv. 3, 5 or 1, 3, 5)

For special texts and ceremonies for use in connection with the Presentation of Our Lord Jesus Christ in the Temple, "Candlemas," another feast taking precedence over the Sunday, see BOS. Suitable hymns include:

28 Angels, from the realms of glory
115 Hail to the Lord who comes
116 O Sion, open wide thy gates
153 Christ, whose glory fills the skies
418 Blest are the pure in heart
442 O very God of very God
477 God himself is with us
545 Hail to the Lord's Anointed
H-209 How lovely are thy dwellings fair
H-215 Lord, let your servant go in peace

On the Last Sunday after the Epiphany the Gospel is the story of the Transfiguration. As the climax of the Christmas-Epiphany Season and the last Sunday before Lent, this day should receive special attention. Suitable hymns include:

54	Alleluia, song of gladness (as the last hymn)
119	O wondrous type! O vision fair
153	Christ, whose glory fills the skies
290	Let all the world in every corner sing
291	Lord of all being, throned afar
346	Fairest Lord Jesus
347	Alleluia! sing to Jesus
367	When morning gilds the skies
599	Ye watchers and ye holy ones
770	Let all the world in every corner sing
H-121, 122	Christ upon the mountain peak

Lenten Season

See the PROPER LITURGIES FOR SPECIAL DAYS (below) for Ash Wednesday, Palm Sunday, Maundy Thursday, Good Friday, and Holy Saturday.

Lent might be set apart from the surrounding festal seasons by beginning the Eucharistic rite with the Great Litany, possibly in procession, or with the Penitential Order.

THE BOOK OF OCCASIONAL SERVICES provides special material for Lenten services relating to the adult catechumenate. It also contains an allocution and directions for the reservation of the Sacrament and the stripping of the altar at the Maundy Thursday liturgy, and two special rites for Lent, the Way of the Cross for Fridays other than Good Friday, and Tenebrae for Wednesday in Holy Week. LESSER FEASTS AND FASTS provides propers for a daily Eucharist in Lent.

Easter Season

For the Great Vigil of Easter see the PROPER LITURGIES FOR SPECIAL DAYS (below).

The Easter season is again, as in the early Church, a season fifty days in length; the Paschal celebration should be sustained throughout this time. Both THE HYMNAL 1940 and HYMNS III contain large sections devoted to Easter. In addition, a number of hymns in the general sections are suitable:

345	The King of love my shepherd is
361	Thou art the Way, to thee alone
763	Welcome, happy morning
765	Come, ye faithful, raise the strain
H-203	Glorious the day when Christ was born
H-218	My shepherd will supply my need
H-224, 225	O love of God, how strong and true
H-232	Sing now with joy unto the Lord
H-234	Sing, ye faithful, sing with gladness
H-236	The gates of death are broken through
H-237	The Lord's my shepherd, I'll not want

Propers are provided in the Prayer Book for a daily Eucharist the first week of Easter and in LESSER FEASTS AND FASTS for the remainder of the Season.

The traditional time for the celebration of the Rogation Days is the Monday, Tuesday, and Wednesday after the Sixth Sunday of Easter. See BOS for the Rogation procession. These days might be marked by the use of the Great Litany, possibly in procession. Suitable hymns include:

101	O Jesus, crowned with all renown
138	We plow the fields and scatter
279	Praise to the Lord, the Almighty, the King of creation
307	Most High, omnipotent, good Lord
308	Let us, with a gladsome mind
497	O God of Bethel, by whose hand
H-187	All creatures of our God and King
H-221	O all ye works of God now come
H-241	This is my Father's world

Suitable hymns for Ascension or the Sunday after the Ascension include:

102	Hail thee, festival day
103	See the Conqueror mounts in triumph

104 Hail the day that sees him rise
105 Look, ye saints, the sight is glorious
106 The head that once was crowned with thorns
347 Alleluia! sing to Jesus
350 Rejoice, the Lord is King
351 Praise the Lord through ev'ry nation
352 Crown him with many crowns
353 Majestic sweetness sits enthroned
354 And have the bright immensities
355 All hail the power of Jesus' Name
356 At the name of Jesus
357 Hail, thou once despisèd Jesus
H-141 A hymn of glory let us sing
H-142 Christ, above all glory seated
H-143, 144 O Lord most high, eternal King
H-230 Rejoice, the Lord is King
H-234 Sing, ye faithful, sing with gladness

For the vigil of Pentecost see PROPER LITURGIES FOR SPECIAL DAYS (below).

Pentecost ranks next after Easter Day as a primary feast day of the Church Year. Many hymns dealing with the Holy Spirit are not suitable for use on the Day of Pentecost because they either do not celebrate the event of the outpouring of the Holy Spirit or they lack a festive character. Some appropriate hymns are:

107 Hail thee, festival day
108 O come, Creator Spirit, come
109 Come, thou Holy Spirit, come
110 Hail thee! Spirit, Lord eternal
111 Spirit of mercy, truth, and love
256 O Spirit of the living God
H-145 To thee, O Comforter divine
H-146 Come down, O Spirit, Love Divine
H-147 Come, Holy Ghost, God and Lord
H-148, 149 Hail this joyful day's return
H-150, 151 Holy Spirit, font of light
H-152 Upon that Whitsun morning

H-153, 154 O Holy Spirit, by whose breath
H-167 O Holy Spirit, enter in
H-207 Holy Ghost, dispel our sadness
H-208 Holy Spirit, ever living
H-223 O Holy Spirit, Lord of grace
H-226 O Spirit of Life, O Spirit of God

The Season after Pentecost

The First Sunday after Pentecost is Trinity Sunday. Suitable hymns include:

266 Holy, Holy, Holy! Lord God Almighty
267 Holy Father, great Creator
268 I bind unto myself today
269 Round the Lord in glory seated
270 Holy, Holy, Holy, Lord
271 Come, thou almighty King
272 Thou, whose almighty word
273 Holy God, we praise thy Name
274 Ancient of Days, who sittest throned in glory
285 The God of Abraham praise
567 Lead us, heav'nly Father, lead us
H-169 Sing praise to our creator
H-190 All glory be to God on high
H-210 How wondrous great, how glorious bright
H-222 O God, we praise thee and confess

The major feast within this Season is All Saints. This day, or the Sunday after All Saints' Day, is one of the five baptismal days of the Church year. A baptismal vigil is provided in the BOS; also included here is a quite different type of service for All Hallows' Eve. Fitting hymns for All Saints' Day are:

124 For thy dear saints, O Lord
125 Hark! the sound of holy voices
126 For all the saints, who from their labors rest
127 How bright these glorious spirits shine
128 The saints of God! their conflict past
129 Joy and triumph everlasting

130 Who are these like stars appearing
397 Let saints on earth in concert sing
569 Lo! what a cloud of witnesses
599 Ye watchers and ye holy ones
600 Ye holy angels bright
H-176 For the bread which thou hast broken
H-194 Remember thy servants, Lord

The final Sundays of the Pentecost Season have an eschatological emphasis. Suitable hymns are:

3 Wake, awake, for night is flying
4 Rejoice, rejoice, believers
8 O Word, that goest forth on high
312 The Lord will come and not be slow
518 Judge eternal, throned in splendor
521 O God of earth and altar
522 Lord Christ, when first thou cam'st to men
525, 784 O Day of God, draw nigh
761 Rejoice, rejoice, believers
H-104 Jesus came — the heavens adoring
H-106 O Savior, open heaven wide
H-107 Once he came in blessing
H-108 Prepare the way, O Zion
H-239 The Lord will come and not be slow

On the Last Sunday after Pentecost the emphasis is on the kingship of Christ. Suitable hymns include:

105 Look, ye saints, the sight is glorious
106 The head that once was crowned with thorns
347 Alleluia! sing to Jesus
350 Rejoice, the Lord is King
351 Praise the Lord through every nation
352 Crown him with many crowns
355 All hail the power of Jesus' Name
356 At the Name of Jesus
357 Hail, thou once despisèd Jesus
H-142 Christ, above all glory seated
H-230 Rejoice, the Lord is King

Proper Liturgies for Special Days

For music see Supplement to HEAE (PROPER LITURGIES FOR SPECIAL DAYS).

Ash Wednesday

(Supplement to HEAE, pp. 240-245)

On Ash Wednesday there should be no music before the service, and the entrance of the ministers should be in silence. The rite begins with the Salutation (*Celebrant*: The Lord be with you. *People*: And also with you.) and the Collect of the Day. A full series of Readings is provided: Old Testament Lesson, Gradual, Epistle, and Gospel. A Tract (see GPAVT) or a Sequence is appropriate between the Epistle and the Gospel. There is a sermon, but the Nicene Creed is omitted. An exhortation and a period of silence follow the sermon.

Prayer (BCP, p. 265). See HEAE or MMC for collect tones.

Psalm 51. The choir or congregation may sing this in unison, antiphonally, or responsorially. If desired, a verse from the Psalm or other verse of Scripture may be used as an Antiphon. It would be fitting for the singing of the Psalm to begin during the imposition of ashes if a large number are receiving the imposition.

Litany of Penitence. If singing the Litany is desired, the tones used for the Great Litany can be adapted for the Suffrages and Responses.

Palm Sunday

(Supplement to HEAE, pp. 246-257; MMC, pp. 28-31)

Pre-service music. A bell or other musical instrument might call the people to silence for the opening anthem. Brass, strings, or other portable musical instruments, later used to accompany the procession, might perform a brief, informal prelude.

Anthem. The text in THE BOOK OF COMMON PRAYER or some other suitable anthem may be sung by the choir. In some situations this anthem might be sung as a simple versicle and response between priest, deacon, or cantor and choir or congregation.

Collect and Reading. See HEAE or MMC for tones.

Blessing of the Palms. Even if the Collect and Reading are said, the form of the blessing of the palms may be sung.

Anthem. The choir may sing this or some other fitting text. Sometimes this anthem could be sung as a simple versicle and response between a priest or a deacon or a cantor and the choir or the congregation.

Procession. Hymns with easily memorized refrains (such as " All glory, laud, and honor," THE HYMNAL 1940, 62) and responsorial psalmody (Ps. 118, VV. 19-29 [See MMC]) are best for the procession. The cantor sings the refrain of either hymn or Psalm; the congregation then repeats it after the cantor and after each verse or group of verses sung by cantor or choir. This avoids the awkwardness for the people of singing from a printed sheet as they process. Portable musical instruments help to give support and keep the group together.

Station. The procession may halt at some landmark on the grounds or at the church entrance for the station Collect, sung to a common collect tone.

Since congregational singing often deteriorates while people climb steps or go through entrances, it is usually wise to end the singing at the door with the station Collect. Then the people enter the church during an instrumental voluntary or choir anthem. "Ride on, ride on in majesty" (THE HYMNAL 1940, 64) is particularly suited here as it points from the entry into Jerusalem to the impending crucifixion, the theme of the lections of the Liturgy of the Word.

The Ministry of the Word begins with the Salutation and Collect. Provisions are made for a full series of readings: Old Testament Lesson, Gradual, Epistle, and Gospel. A Tract or Sequence is appropriate between the Epistle and Gospel. Appropriate hymns include:

64 Ride on! ride on in majesty
68 Alone thou goest forth, O Lord
H-217 My song is love unknown

Passion Gospel. Laypersons may read or chant the Passion Gospel. For traditional music for singing it, see THE PASSIONS, published by Music for Liturgy, 175 West 72nd St., New York, NY 10023 (RSV) and CHANTS OF THE PASSION ACCORDING TO MATTHEW, MARK, LUKE AND JOHN arranged for singing by Jan Kern (GIA Publications, 7404 South Mason, Bedford Park, IL 60638) (New American Bible).

After the reading of the Gospel and for the remainder of the service, all hymns, anthems, and instrumental music should be devoted to the crucifixion. For example, it is highly inappropriate after the Gospel to use a text such as "All glory, laud, and honor" or instrumental music with Palm Sunday entry associations. Useful hymns include:

68 Alone thou goest forth, O Lord
71 Ah, holy Jesus, how hast thou offended
75 O sacred head, sore wounded
337 When I survey the wondrous cross
338 Behold the Lamb of God
340 We sing the praise of him who died

The Nicene Creed and the Confession of Sin seem redundant and should probably be omitted after use of the Liturgy of the Palms.

Maundy Thursday

The two primary emphases of the Maundy Thursday rite are the institution of the Eucharist and the "maundy," the washing of feet with its attendent command to love one another. Particularly fitting are hymns referring to the institution of the Eucharist and versions of traditional maundy texts.

193 Sion, praise thy Savior, singing
199 Now, my tongue, the mystery telling
H-202 God is love, and where true love is
H-247 Where charity and love prevail
H-248 Where true love and charity are found

The liturgy begins in the usual manner. Even though it is Lent, it has been traditional in some areas to sing the Gloria in excelsis or some other song of praise in the entrance rite, possibly with the ringing of bells; then organ, bells, and other musical instruments are silent until the Eucharist of the Easter Vigil. Often this is not practical. Also, many people feel strongly that use of the Kyrie or Trisagion instead of a song of praise is more in keeping with the Maundy Thursday rite.

Washing of feet. During the washing of feet, following the sermon, the choir or cantor may sing the anthems provided in THE BOOK OF COMMON PRAYER or some other suitable ones. The congregation should not sing a hymn or psalm at this point for their total attention should be directed to the washing of feet. However, a cantor or choir might sing a hymn with a congregational refrain.

H-202 God is love, and where true love is
H-213 Jesu, Jesu, fill us with your love
H-248 Where true love and charity are found

After the washing of the feet, the service continues with the Prayers of the People and proceeds in the usual manner through the postcommunion prayer. Then a Dismissal may follow, or the congregation may remain for the removal of the Sacrament to the place of repose and/or the stripping of the altar.

Stripping of the altar. If the stripping of the altar is a public ceremony, it follows the postcommunion prayer (and hymn). It may occur in silence, or Psalm 22 could accompany it. Verse 17b and c of that Psalm, "They divide my garments among them; they cast lots for my clothing," is an appropriate antiphon. After this, the congregation may leave or remain for a vigil. An instrumental postlude would not be appropriate. See BOS for additional provisions for Maundy Thursday.

Good Friday

(Supplement to HEAE, pp. 258-276; MMC, p. 31)

On Good Friday there should be no music before the service; the entrance of the ministers should be silent and should be followed by an appreciable period of silent prayer. The liturgy begins with a special Acclamation and the Collect of the Day. A full series of readings is provided: Old Testament Lesson, Gradual, Epistle, and Gospel. A Tract or Sequence between the Epistle and Gospel is appropriate.

Passion Gospel. For traditional music for this, see above (Palm Sunday Passion Gospel).

Hymn. On Good Friday a hymn may follow the sermon.

67 See the destined day arise
68 Alone thou goest forth, O Lord
71 Ah, holy Jesus, how hast thou offended
75 O sacred head, sore wounded
336 In the cross of Christ I glory
337 When I survey the wondrous cross
338 Behold the Lamb of God
340 We sing the praise of him who died
342 Jesus, Name all names above
777 In the cross of Christ I glory
778 Jesus, Name all names above

Solemn Collects. For traditional music, see HEAE, pages 264-270.

Anthems and/or hymns. Anthems (three are provided and others may also be used) may be read or sung after the bringing in of a wooden cross. "Sing, my tongue, the glorious battle" (66, 764) or some other suitable hymn extolling the glory of the cross is then sung. Particularly suited are:

63 The royal banners forward go
71 Ah, holy Jesus, how hast thou offended
75 O sacred head, sore wounded
336 In the cross of Christ I glory
337 When I survey the wondrous cross
338 Behold the Lamb of God
340 We sing the praise of him who died
342 Jesus, Name all names above
777 In the cross of Christ I glory
778 Jesus, Name all names above

After the anthems and the hymn have been sung before the cross, it is probably best not to use any more music in the service. The ministers and people depart in silence. In some situations, however, appropriate hymns, psalms or anthems during the ministration of Communion might be effective.

Holy Saturday

On Holy Saturday there should be no music before the service; the entrance of the clergy should be silent. The rite begins with the Collect of the Day. A full series of readings is given: Old Testament Lesson, Gradual, Epistle, and Gospel. A Tract or a Sequence is fitting between the Epistle and Gospel. Hymn 83, "O sorrow deep," of THE HYMNAL 1940 is a good choice for a sequence.

Anthem. The anthem "In the midst of life" (BCP, pp. 484 or 492) may be sung by priest, deacon, cantor, or choir. The form on page 492 is well suited for congregational singing of the refrain with cantor or choir singing the verses.

Lord's Prayer and Grace. The Lord's Prayer may be monotoned, or a setting such as 705 or 722 in THE HYMNAL 1940 or those on pages 17, 31, or 40 in CHURCH HYMNAL SERIES I or those in CME or MMC may be used. The Grace (BCP, pp. 59 or 102) may be monotoned.

The Great Vigil of Easter

(Supplement to HEAE, pp. 278-320; MMC, p. 32)

Lighting of the Paschal Candle. The opening address may be monotoned, and the Collect may be sung to a common collect tone. (See HEAE.)

Acclamation. The Acclamation is sung or said three times. It is sung at a higher pitch each time. For additional information see HEAE.

Exsultet. Even if little else is sung, this should be. If a deacon is not available, a priest or the best cantor available should sing it.

The Liturgy of the Word. The address of the celebrant may be monotoned, the Lessons and Collects sung to common tones. Great restraint must be exercised in the use of psalms, canticles, and hymns other than those listed as responses to the Lessons. This is not an Easter festival carol service, but rather a vigil of readings set off by silences and responses in the words of Scripture and by solemn prayers. It is probably best for the congregation to sit during the Psalms. Responsorial singing is recommended. If accompaniment is necessary, recorders, harpsichord, or other quiet instruments are preferred, thus reserving the organ, bells, brass and other loud instruments for the initial song of praise at the Eucharist.

Holy Baptism. A suitable psalm, such as Psalm 42, or a hymn may accompany the procession to the font. Singing the Prayers for the Candidates, the Thanksgiving over the Water and the Consecration of the Chrism and singing or monotoning other prayers or forms is appropriate. (See HEAE or MMC.) Psalm 23 or some other psalm or hymn may be sung at the time of a procession to the front of the church after the Baptism. In the rite of Confirmation, Reception, or Reaffirmation, one may sing the prayers.

Renewal of Baptismal Vows. It is appropriate to sing the concluding prayer.

At the Eucharist. Bells and/or an instrumental fanfare are suitable at the lighting of the altar and chancel candles. The acclamation of the celebrant and the response of the people may be repeated several times. If sung, each repetition might be at a higher pitch.

Canticle. After the restrained psalmody of the vigil, the canticle setting should be popular, festive, and congregational. If the congregation can join heartily in a setting of Pascha nostrum or Te Deum laudamus, because of the references in the texts to the resurrection, one of these would be more appropriate to the occasion than Gloria in excelsis. The organ, silent until this point in the rite, might have brass, percussion and/or bell accompaniment.

Ministry of the Word. The Epistle and Gospel may be sung, separated by a sung Alleluia and Psalm 114 or some other suitable psalm or hymn. Hymn 97, "Christians, to the Paschal victim," is a traditional Easter Sequence. The Nicene Creed is omitted. The sermon is followed by (the Baptism or Renewal of Baptismal Vows and) the Prayers of the People and the Peace.

The hymns, psalms, or anthems at the Offertory, during the Communion, and before and/or after the postcommunion prayer should stress the passover event. The following hymns are suggested:

89	At the Lamb's high feast we sing
94	Come, ye faithful, raise the strain
96	The day of resurrection
97	Christians, to the Paschal victim
H-136, 137	The Lamb's high banquet called to share
H-138	Through the Red Sea brought at last

Note that "Alleluia, alleluia" may be added to the Dismissal and its response from the Easter Vigil through the Day of Pentecost. For music see HEAE and MMC.

The Vigil of Pentecost

The Service of Light. The Vigil of Pentecost begins with the Order of Worship for the Evening. A musical prelude or processional is not appropriate. For the music for the Opening Acclamation, see BC, C-27C, or HEAE, page 206. If used, the short Lesson may be sung to the tone provided in HEAE, page 206, or MMC, page 34, or monotoned. A common collect tone may be used for the Prayer for Light. If the Vigil is kept on Saturday evening, the first of the prayers on BCP, page 110 is especially fitting. See BOS for a traditional lucernaria text for Pentecost. A cantor or choir may sing another appropriate anthem or psalm. Another canticle or hymn may replace Phos hilaron.

The Ministry of the Word. The Ministry of the Word begins with the Salutation and Collect of the Day, which may be sung to a common collect tone. At least three Lessons precede the Gospel. Any hymn substituted for a psalm or canticle prior to the Alleluia or Sequence should invoke the Holy Spirit. For translations of Veni Creator Spiritus see:

108	O come, Creator Spirit, come
217	Come, Holy Ghost, our souls inspire
218	Come, Holy Ghost, Creator blest
371	Creator Spirit, by whose aid
H-146	Come down, O Spirit, Love Divine
H-153, 154	O Holy Spirit, by whose breath

For translations of Veni Sancte Spiritus, the traditional Sequence for Pentecost, see:

109 Come, thou Holy Spirit, come
H-150, 151 Holy Spirit, font of light

Holy Baptism. The procession to the font may be accompanied by the singing of an appropriate psalm, such as Psalm 42, or a baptismal hymn invoking the Holy Spirit.

H-165 Spirit of God, unleashed on earth
H-166 Descend, O Spirit, purging flame
H-167 O Holy Spirit, enter in
H-168 Praise and thanksgiving be our creator
H-171 This is the Spirit's entry now

It is appropriate to sing the Prayers for the Candidates, the Thanksgiving over Water, and the Consecration of the Chrism, and to sing or monotone other prayers or forms as well. Psalm 23, some other related psalm, or a hymn celebrating the outpouring of the Holy Spirit in Baptism (See HYMNS III, H-169, "Sing praise to our creator," and H-170, "We know that Christ is raised and dies no more.") may be sung at the procession to the front of the church following the Baptism. If the rite of Confirmation, Reception, or Reaffirmation is administered, it is suitable to sing the prayers of that rite.

Renewal of Baptismal Vows. The concluding prayer may be sung. The Prayers of the People and the Peace follow the Renewal or Baptism.

At the Eucharist. The hymns, psalms, and anthems at the Offertory, during the Communion, and before and/or after the postcommunion prayer, should be festive.

Suggested hymns are:

107 Hail thee, festival day
111 Spirit of mercy, truth, and love
256 O Spirit of the living God
H-145 To thee, O Comforter divine
H-147 Come, Holy Ghost, God and Lord

H-148, 149 Hail this joyful day's return
H-152 Upon that Whitsun morning
H-208 Holy Spirit, ever living
H-223 O Holy Spirit, Lord of grace
H-226 O Spirit of Life, O Spirit of God

Note that "Alleluia, alleluia" may be added to the Dismissal and its response.

Planning Music for Holy Baptism

The Prayer Book provides a special entrance rite for Holy Baptism. Sentences of Scripture sung or said responsively take the place of the Kyrie, Trisagion, or song of praise. For music, see HEAE or MMC. At the Great Vigil of Easter or the Vigil of Pentecost, this entrance rite is not used. These primary baptismal times have their own special entrance rites with a service of light and a special Ministry of the Word. See BOS for baptismal vigils for the First Sunday after Epiphany and All Saints, and for a "Vigil on the Eve of Baptism."

Procession to the Font. This may precede or follow the presentation and examination of candidates and the baptismal covenant. Psalm 42, some other suitable psalm, or a baptismal hymn may be sung during the procession.

268 I bind unto myself today
404 My God, accept my heart this day
H-164 All who believe and are baptized
H-165 Spirit of God, unleashed on earth
H-166 Descend, O Spirit, purging flame
H-167 O Holy Spirit, enter in
H-168 Praise and thanksgiving be to our creator
H-171 This is the Spirit's entry now

Prayers for the Candidates. Music for these prayers is in HEAE or MMC. The procession may move to the font during the singing of these prayers. The celebrant's concluding prayer may be sung to a common collect tone.

Thanksgiving over the Water and Consecration of the Chrism. For the music, see HEAE, pages 236-238. It is appropriate to sing other prayers to a common collect tone and also to monotone other forms.

Procession to the Altar. Psalm 23, some other suitable psalm, or a hymn may be sung.

H-169 Sing praise to our creator
H-170 We know that Christ is raised
H-172 We praise you, Lord, for Jesus Christ
H-131 Come away to the skies

Confirmation, Reception, or Reaffirmation. If one of these rites is administered, the prayers may be sung.

Peace. For music, see HEAE or MMC. After the Peace, the Eucharistic rite continues with the Prayers of the People or the Offertory.

Planning Music for The Holy Eucharist

Quite early in Church history a classic shape evolved for the Eucharistic rite. The Liturgy of the Word consisted of: 1. Old Testament Lesson(s), 2. Psalmody, 3. New Testament Lesson(s), 4. A reading from the Gospels, 5. Homily, 6. Prayers of the People, and 7. The Peace. A four-action shape developed for the Liturgy of the Table: 1. The preparation of the Table, 2. The Great Thanksgiving, 3. The Breaking of the Bread, and 4. The giving of the Bread and Wine. Over the years these basic structures were somewhat obscured, and certain elements were lost. The new BOOK OF COMMON PRAYER restores the basic components of both the Liturgy of the Word and the Liturgy of the Table. These elements should stand out. Other items in the liturgy should function as preparation and reinforcement for the basic elements.

The Entrance Rite

The real beginning of the liturgy is the first Lesson. That which precedes this reading is often called "the entrance rite." It serves to call the congregation together and set the stage for the readings and all that follows. In planning, it is best to begin with the Ministry of the Word and move on to the Holy Communion. After these are worked out, plan an entrance rite which best prepares the people. This rite must not be so lengthy or so emotionally demanding that it exhausts the people; rather it should call them together and prepare them for hearing the proclamation of the Word.

Certain days or occasions have their own entrance rites. For other occasions there are often five available options; an entrance song may precede the first three.

Prelude. Congregational participation can be enhanced if the time immediately before the entrance song is used to familiarize them with new music in the rite. The music itself or preludes based on it will serve this purpose.

Occasionally it is advisable to have a congregational hymn and service music practice just before the prelude. In addition to music for teaching, musical offerings by instrumentalists, choir, or vocalists are also appropriate.

Entrance Song. A hymn, psalm, or anthem may be used at the entrance of the ministers. The choir should be in place prior to this song, or at least well into the nave when the singing begins. Although a psalm or anthem may be used sometimes, this song should be ideally a familiar hymn of praise related to the theme of the Lessons for the day. When this is impossible, a seasonal hymn is suitable; if not a seasonal hymn, then a general hymn of praise.

> *Option I:* The normal use from Christmas Day through the Feast of the Epiphany, on Sundays from Easter Day through the Day of Pentecost, on all the days of Easter Week, and on Ascension Day; and permitted at other times except in Advent and Lent (BCP, p. 406).

Opening Acclamation. Music is given in HEAE or MMC.

Collect for Purity. This Collect, required in Rite One but optional in Rite Two, may be sung in the same manner as the Collect of the Day. That would not be inappropriate with a sung Opening Acclamation, Kyrie, Trisagion, or song of praise. In Rite Two, the Collect for Purity interrupts the movement from the entrance song and Opening Acclamation to the song of praise.

Kyrie or Trisagion. In Rite One, Kyrie or Trisagion may be used even on those occasions calling for a song of praise.

Song of Praise. Gloria in excelsis is an excellent choice for Christmastide. The Daily Office canticles are desirable alternatives for other seasons. Te Deum laudamus is appropriate for the Easter Season, saints' days, and Trinity Sunday; Pascha nostrum or Dignus es for the Easter Season; Benedictus Dominus Deus or Surge, illuminare or Magna et mirabilia for Epiphany; Magnificat for Marian feasts, *et al.* (See Appendix I.) For music see CHS 1, CME, and BC.

Option II: The normal option for Advent and Lent, permissible at other times.

Opening Acclamation. Music is provided in HEAE or MMC.

Collect for Purity. This Collect, required in Rite One but optional in Rite Two, may be sung in the same manner as the Collect of the Day. It would not be inappropriate if the Opening Acclamation and the Kyrie or Trisagion are sung.

Kyrie or Trisagion. Kyrie may be sung or said in a three-fold, six-fold, or nine-fold form. Trisagion may be sung or said antiphonally and/or three times in accordance with Eastern custom. For music see CHS 1 and CME.

Option III: The use of A Penitential Order (Rite One, pp. 319-321; Rite Two, pp. 351-353), appropriate in Lent and on certain other occasions.

Opening Acclamation. Music for it appears in HEAE or MMC.

Kyrie eleison, Trisagion, Gloria in excelsis or other song of praise. See Option I or Option II (above).

Option IV: The use of the Great Litany (BCP, pp. 148-153), appropriate in Lent and on certain other occasions. When used as an entrance rite, it is concluded with the Kyrie on page 153.

Option V: The use of An Order of Worship for the Evening (BCP, pp. 108-112). The Order of Worship for the Evening, ending with the Phos hilaron, may be used in place of all that precedes the Salutation and Collect of the Day. For music see MOWE, HEAE or MMC.

The Ministry of the Word

Salutation and Collect. Two tones for the Collect are provided in HEAE and MMC.

Old Testament Lesson. If the Lesson is sung, the announcement and conclusion should also be sung. See HEAE or MMC for the tone.

Silence. A period of silence may be observed after the reading.

Gradual. Whereas other psalms are accompaniments to actions, this psalm has a unique rationale and integrity. Sometimes the early Church Fathers spoke of it as the Lesson from the Psalms. Traditionally, the congregation remains seated while the psalm is sung responsorially, with the cantor singing the verses and the congregation repeating the antiphon after each verse or group of verses. (This presupposes a teaching session prior to the first time that it is used in a congregation.) It is not traditional to use Gloria Patri after the Gradual. For music, see GPAVT.

In some congregations it may be desirable to make occasional use of plainchant or Anglican settings of the Gradual or of a metrical setting of the Psalm. (See HYMNS III for a listing of the metrical psalms included in that book as well as in THE HYMNAL 1940.) In some situations it may be well on occasion to substitute for the Proper Psalm an Invitatory Psalm or an Old Testament canticle familiar through use at the Daily Office.

New Testament Lesson. If this is sung, the announcement and conclusion are also sung. See HEAE or MMC for the tone.

Silence. A period of silence may be kept after the reading.

Alleluia or Tract. An acclamation consisting of alleluias with a verse of Scripture has traditionally preceded the Gospel in the West. A psalm, without Gloria Patri, known as the Tract, has been a traditional substitute for the Alleluia and Verse during Lent. See GPAVT for settings of Alleluias and Tracts.

Sequence. A hymn may replace the Alleluia or Tract at this point. It should sum up, highlight or respond to the Epistle or anticipate the Gospel. Both an Alleluia and a Sequence may be used on occasion.

Gospel. See HEAE or MMC for the tone. The Gloria tibi and Laus tibi should not be sung unless the announcement and the conclusion are sung.

There is no longer permission to sing a hymn between the Gospel and the sermon; nothing should intervene between the people's response to the Gospel and the initial sentence of the sermon. Also, there is no longer blanket permission to follow the sermon with a hymn. It is fitting to have there a period of silence or to lead directly into the Creed or the Prayers of the People.

Creed. The Creed is required only on Sundays and on other major feasts. On the great baptismal days (Easter, Pentecost, All Saints' Day or the Sunday after All Saints' Day, and The Baptism of our Lord) when there are no baptismal candidates, the Renewal of Baptismal Vows (BCP, pp. 292-294) may take the place of the Nicene Creed. If the congregation knows a setting of the Creed, it is suitable to sing it. It is not good form for the organist to play during the congregation's monotoning of the Creed.

Prayers of the People. See HEAE or MMC for the tones for Forms I and V.

Concluding Collect. The concluding Collect may be sung to the tone of the Collect of the Day, even though the petitions have been said, or vice versa.

Peace. See HEAE or MMC for the tone. The organist should allow adequate time for the exchange of the Peace but avoid an undue lag.

The Holy Communion

Offertory Sentence. It is often more effective for the organist simply to begin a hymn, anthem, or organ voluntary than for the priest to say a sentence of Scripture to initiate the Offertory, especially if the people are enthusiastic in exchanging the Peace.

Hymn, psalm, or anthem. Music during the preparation of the Table and the placing on it of the bread, wine, alms, and other offerings is in itself an offering. It should serve as a meditative aid to the people, preparing them for their participation in the Great Thanksgiving. The music should be restrained in length and emotional content. Triumphal processions and the saying or singing of a presentation Sentence are highly inappropriate, for the Great Thanksgiving is, in itself, the verbalization of the offering and the climax toward which the Offertory moves. If the action of the Offertory is not completed by the conclusion of the hymn, anthem, or voluntary, a period of silence is in order.

The Great Thanksgiving. See HEAE or MMC for settings for the Sursum corda, the Prefaces, and the conclusion of the Great Thanksgiving. The older tradition of singing the entire Eucharistic Prayer, now being restored, is commendable.

Even if the celebrant sings no portion of the Eucharistic Prayer, the people should sing the Sanctus and the Memorial Acclamation. (See CHS I and CME.)

Lord's Prayer. Congregational singing of the Lord's Prayer is appropriate, at least occasionally, especially if the Eucharistic Prayer has been sung. For settings, see CHS I, CME and MMC.

Fraction Anthem. The Bread is broken, and there is a period of silence. An anthem is appropriate after the silence which follows the Breaking of The Bread. Two texts appear in THE BOOK OF COMMON PRAYER (p. 337 for Rite One and pp. 364 and 407 for Rite Two). Additional seasonal texts are provided in BOS.

It is not desirable to use both Pascha nostrum and Agnus Dei. Musical settings for the former are in HEAE and MMC. Settings for both are in CHS I and CME. Dignus es is appropriate on occasion, and Pascha nostrum is suitable during the Easter Season. For settings, see

BC. Some appropriate hymns referring to the breaking of bread are:

- 207 Come, risen Lord, and deign to be our guest
- 213 Shepherd of souls, refresh and bless
- H-173 Come, risen Lord, and deign to be our guest

The omission of a Fraction Anthem, on occasion, is often highly effective, as is the substitution of an instrumental fanfare.

Invitation. See HEAE for the proper music.

Hymn, psalm, or anthem during Communion. This is a fitting time for a choir anthem. Responsorial psalmody is traditional here. It works well because it enables the people to continue singing as they move to and from the Communion station. Certain hymns with refrains can also be used. Canticles particularly appropriate to the season may also be used (see Appendix I). Music of great length or dramatic quality which is inappropriate at the offering, where music should lead up to the climactic prayer of the rite, is often well suited to the Communion procession. Joyous music is especially good. Historically, great psalms of praise, especially Psalms 145, 148, and 150, have been associated with this point in the rite.

Hymn. A hymn is often needed prior to the postcommunion prayer to get the congregation back on their feet and to cover the ablutions or removal of the elements. A hymn associated with this moment in historic liturgies is appropriate.

- 201 Strengthen for service, Lord
- 492 From glory to glory advancing, we praise thee, O Lord
- H-175 Completed, Lord, the Holy Mysteries

A hymn proper to the season or related to the day's lections or a general hymn of praise may also be used.

Postcommunion prayer. If desired, this prayer may be monotoned.

Hymn. This is the last point within the rite for a hymn. The choir should remain in place throughout the hymn to provide congregational support. Ideally, this hymn should be very familiar.

Blessing and/or Dismissal. A blessing is required in Rite One and a dismissal in Rite Two. "Alleluia, Alleluia" may be added to the Dismissal throughout the Great Fifty Days. See the HEAE or MMC for music for blessings and dismissals. See BOS for seasonal blessings and Lenten prayers over the people.

Postlude. The music at the exit of the clergy and people should derive from that hymn or text which best sums up the service. The time might be used to familiarize the people with a tune intended for future use. The choir, like the congregation, should leave informally.

Planning Music for the Pastoral Offices

Confirmation, Reception, or Reaffirmation of Baptismal Vows

THE BOOK OF COMMON PRAYER provides a special entrance rite for use at Confirmation, Reception, or Reaffirmation of Baptismal Vows. Sentences of Scripture are sung or said responsively in place of the Kyrie, Trisagion, or song of praise. For music, see HEAE or MMC. At the Great Vigil of Easter or the Vigil of Pentecost this entrance rite is not used, for those primary times of Baptism and Renewal of Baptismal Vows have their own special entrance rites with a service of light and a special Ministry of the Word.

The prayers of the rite may be sung. For the music of the petitions see HEAE or MMC. The other prayers may be sung to a common collect tone. For the music for the Peace, see HEAE or MMC.

After the Peace, the Eucharistic rite continues with the Prayers of the People or the Offertory.

A Form of Commitment to Christian Service

This rite must be tailored to each individual situation. Occasionally it may be appropriate to include a hymn or psalm as a portion of the statement of intention and/or to monotone or sing the prayers to a common collect tone.

Celebration and Blessing of a Marriage

The celebration and blessing of a marriage is a sacramental rite of the Church; the music should reflect this. As at other rites of the Church, the canon and rubrics govern the choices.

Prelude. Preludes based on hymns or service music to be used within the rite are especially appropriate. Since congregations at weddings often include a large number of people unfamiliar with some of the hymns and service music, participation is greatly enhanced by the organist's playing the hymns and service music or preludes based on them. Instrumentalists, a choir, or soloists may also make musical offerings at this time.

Entrance hymn, psalm, anthem, or instrumental music. A strong general hymn of praise is probably better at the entrance than any of the hymns in the marriage section of either THE HYMNAL 1940 or HYMNS III. Some suitable hymns are:

276 Now thank we all our God
278 All people that on earth do dwell
279 Praise to the Lord, the Almighty, the King of creation
280 God, my King, thy might confessing
281 Joyful, joyful, we adore thee
282 Praise, my soul, the King of heaven
285 The God of Abraham praise
287 Give praise and glory unto God
384 Christ is made the sure foundation
769 Joyful, joyful, we adore thee
780 Christ is made the sure foundation
786 Rejoice, ye pure in heart
H-187 All creatures of our God and King
H-190 All glory be to God on high
H-220 New songs of celebration render
H-221 O all ye works of God now come
H-222 O God, we praise thee and confess
H-228 Praise the Lord! ye heavens adore him
H-230 Rejoice, the Lord is King
H-231 Sing, all creation

H-233 Sing praise to God who reigns above
H-234 Sing, ye faithful, sing with gladness
H-235 Tell out, my soul
H-243 To God with gladness sing

Appropriate psalms for the entrance include the Invitatory Psalms 95 and 100 (see BC) and the psalms appointed for use at a wedding — 67, 127, and 128. Other useful Psalms are 148 and 150. Several collections of organ music contain music suited for use at the entrance:

PARISH ORGANIST — WEDDING MUSIC VOLUME IX. Concordia.

WEDDING MUSIC, I AND II. Concordia.

WEDDING MUSIC, I AND II. (Ed. David Johnson) Augsburg.

A BOOK OF WEDDING PIECES. OUP.

A SECOND BOOK OF WEDDING PIECES. (Ed. C.H. Trevor & Christopher Morris) OUP.

CEREMONIAL MUSIC — PURCELL. (Ed. E. Power Biggs) Mercury (Presser).

CEREMONIAL MUSIC I AND II. OUP.

Various trumpet voluntaries by English composers (Boyce, Stanley, et al.) are especially useful.

Hymn, psalm, or anthem. A hymn, psalm, or anthem may follow the Declaration of Consent (and Giving in Marriage). A hymn from the wedding section of either THE HYMNAL 1940 or HYMNS III would be appropriate:

214 O perfect Love, all human thought transcending
215 Lord, who at Cana's wedding feast
216 May the grace of Christ our Savior
H-179 Dear Father, in thy house today
H-180 O thou whose favor hallows all occasions

Other suitable hymns are:

363 Lord of all hopefulness, Lord of all joy
497 O God of Bethel, by whose hand
504 Our Father, by whose Name

The Ministry of the Word. See HEAE or MMC for tones for the Salutation and Collect. There is provision for a full series of lections: Old Testament Lesson, Gradual, Epistle, and Gospel. An Alleluia, Tract, or Sequence is appropriate between the Epistle and Gospel. (See GPAVT.)

Prayers and blessing. For music see MMC II.

Peace. For the music for the Peace, see HEAE or MMC.

At the Eucharist. The Offertory would be an appropriate time for a meditative hymn, anthem, or solo if desired. Suitable hymns include:

216 May the grace of Christ our Savior
363 Lord of all hopefulness, Lord of all joy
497 O God of Bethel, by whose hand
504 Our Father, by whose Name
H-179 Dear Father, in thy house today
H-180 O thou whose favor hallows all occasions
H-202 God is love, and where true love is
H-247 Where charity and love prevail

Several collections contain suitable vocal music:

WEDDING BLESSINGS. Concordia.

SACRED SONGS. Bach, Concordia.

WEDDING SONGS. F. Peeters, Peters.

WEDDING SONGS. Jan Bender, Concordia.

THREE WEDDING SONGS. Robert Powell, Concordia.

THREE WEDDING SOLOS. G. Winston Cassler, Augsburg.

BELOVED LET US LOVE. R. Proulx, Augsburg.

The rite continues with the Great Thanksgiving. The Sursum corda, Preface, Sanctus, Memorial Acclamation, and conclusion of the Eucharistic Prayer may be sung. (See HEAE, MMC, CHS I, and CME.) The Lord's Prayer, Fraction Anthem, and Invitation to Communion may also be sung. (See HEAE, MMC, CHS I, and CME.) Psalm 23 is appropriate at the Communion, as are hymns such as 345, "The King of love my shepherd is" (vv. 1, 2, 5, and 6), H-218, "My shepherd will supply my need," and H-237, "The Lord's my shepherd." Appropriate hymns for use before or after the postcommunion prayer include 201, "Strengthen for service, Lord," and H-211, "If thou but suffer God to guide thee."

Hymn, psalm, anthem, or instrumental music. A hymn, psalm, or anthem may be sung or instrumental music played as the wedding party leaves the church. Appropriate hymns are:

216 May the grace of Christ our Savior
276 Now thank we all our God
279 Praise to the Lord, the Almighty, the King of creation
280 God, my King, thy might confessing
281 Joyful, joyful, we adore thee
282 Praise, my soul, the King of heaven
285 The God of Abraham praise
287 Give praise and glory unto God
497 O God of Bethel, by whose hand
769 Joyful, joyful, we adore thee
H-187 All creatures of our God and King
H-228 Praise the Lord! ye heavens adore him
H-233 Sing praise to God who reigns above

Suitable instrumental music is in the collections listed above and in J.S. Bach, ORGELBÜCHLEIN (various editions) ("In thee is gladness," "If thou but suffer God to guide thee").

Blessing of a Civil Marriage. Music appropriate for use at the Celebration and Blessing of a Marriage is also suited to the blessing of a civil marriage. Also appropriate is the hymn for use at the renewal of marriage promises, H-181, "O Father blest, we ask of you."

An Order for Marriage. Music appropriate for the Celebration and Blessing of a Marriage should constitute the norm for music used in this order.

Thanksgiving for the Birth or Adoption of a Child

On occasion it may be appropriate to sing the Magnificat or Psalm, to monotone or sing the prayers to a common collect tone, and to sing the blessing. The music for the Aaronic blessing in HEAE and MMC can be adapted for this blessing.

Ministration to the Sick

When used as a public service, the Ministry of the Word and the Holy Communion may include music suitable for a regular Eucharistic rite. Hymns stressing the healing power of God are fitting:

157 Father, we praise thee, now the night is over
272 Thou, whose almighty word
279 Praise to the Lord, the Almighty, the King of creation
293 O bless the Lord, my soul
325 O for a thousand tongues to sing
515 From thee all skill and science flow
516 Father, whose will is life and good
517 Thine arm, O Lord, in days of old
776 O for a thousand tongues to sing
H-145 To thee, O Comforter divine
H-212 I to the hills will lift mine eyes
H-218 My shepherd will supply my need
H-211 If thou but suffer God to guide thee

The prayers of the Laying on of Hands and Anointing (Part II) may be monotoned or sung to a common collect tone. Singing the blessing of oil for the Anointing of the Sick gives it a desired emphasis, whether it is used within this rite or, as is more desirable, at a principal Sunday Eucharist.

Ministration at the Time of Death

Litany at the Time of Death. Within a monastic or collegiate community, it may be appropriate to sing the Litany at the Time of Death (See MMC II). This Litany may also be used within the Vigil (see below).

Prayers for a Vigil. In some circumstances it may be possible to use music at the Vigil from the Vigil rite (see MMC II) or the Litany at the Time of Death (see above) or prayers from the Burial of the Dead (see below). Psalms appointed for use in the burial rite might also be sung.

Responsorial singing of the psalms would probably be most practicable since it eliminates the need for books or sheets of music.

Burial of the Dead

The same principles as those for any other regular or proper liturgies apply to the choice of music for a burial.

Prelude. Preludes based on hymns or service music to appear within the rite are particularly appropriate. Since a congregation gathered for a burial includes a number of persons unfamiliar with some hymns and service music, participation will improve greatly if the organist familiarizes them with the music by using it or preludes based on it. Instrumentalists, a choir, or soloists may also make a musical offering.

Opening anthems. The minister, the minister and the people, a cantor, or a choir sing or say one or more anthems. For music see MMC II. In Rite Two a hymn, psalm, or other suitable anthem may be sung in place of anthems in BCP. Suitable hymns include:

289 O God, our help in ages past
361 Thou art the Way, to thee alone
397 Let saints on earth in concert sing
551 A mighty fortress is our God
564 How firm a foundation, ye saints of the Lord
589 O what their joy and their glory must be
785 How firm a foundation, ye saints of the Lord
H-133 I know that my Redeemer lives
H-212 I to the hills will lift mine eyes
H-216 Lord, thou hast searched me
H-218 My shepherd will supply my need
H-237 The Lord's my shepherd, I'll not want

Salutation and Collect. For the common collect tones see HEAE or MMC.

Liturgy of the Word. A full series of readings is provided: Old Testament Lesson, Gradual (or hymn or canticle), New Testament Lesson, Tract (or Sequence or canticle) and Gospel. (See GPAVT, "Burial of the Dead" and "For the Departed.") Suitable hymns include:

88 Jesus lives! thy terrors now
91 The strife is o'er, the battle done
289 O God, our help in ages past
361 Thou art the Way, to thee alone
445 Christ leads me through no darker rooms
H-133 I know that my Redeemer lives
H-212 I to the hills will lift mine eyes
H-216 Lord, thou hast searched me
H-218 My shepherd will supply my need
H-237 The Lord's my shepherd, I'll not want

Prayers. For music, see MMC II. The concluding Collect of Rite Two may be sung to a common collect tone.

At the Eucharist. The Eucharist commences with the Peace and continues as usual (with the Preface for the Commemoration of the Dead if a Eucharistic Prayer allowing a Proper Preface is used) until the special postcommunion prayer. Suitable hymns at the Offertory or at the Communion or before the postcommunion prayer include:

345 The King of love my shepherd is
361 Thou art the Way, to thee alone
397 Let saints on earth in concert sing
H-188 All my hope on God is founded
H-211 If thou but suffer God to guide thee
H-218 My shepherd will supply my need
H-237 The Lord's my shepherd, I'll not want

Commendation. For a musical setting of the anthem, see HYMNS III, H-183, "Give rest, O Christ, to your servant(s) with your saints." The commendation "Into your hands. . ." may be sung to the setting in MMC II or it may be monotoned.

Dismissal. For music see HEAE or MMC .

Hymn, anthem, or canticle. For music for the final anthem, see:

H-182 May choirs of angels lead you
H-184 Into paradise may the angels lead you
H-185, 186 May angels lead you into Paradise

Suitable hymns include:

91 The strife is o'er, the battle done
126 For all the saints, who from their labors rest
551 A mighty fortress is our God
585 Jerusalem, my happy home
589 O what their joy and their glory must be
599 Ye watchers and ye holy ones
600 Ye holy angels bright
H-133 I know that my Redeemer lives
H-205 Guide me, O thou great Jehovah
H-228 Praise the Lord! ye heavens adore him
H-234 Sing, ye faithful, sing with gladness

For settings of the recommended canticles, see BC, C-21—24, 68—80 (Rite One), C-43—46, 142—157 (Rite Two).

The Committal

Anthem. The minister, cantor, or choir may sing or say the anthem. For music see MMC II.

The Committal. For music see MMC II.

Prayers. The Lord's Prayer may be monotoned, and other prayers sung to a collect tone.

Dismissal. For music see MMC II.

An Order for Burial

For suggestions for appropriate music, see the Burial of the Dead (above).

Planning Music for Episcopal Services

An Ordination (Bishop, Priest, or Deacon)

Prelude. People at an ordination rite normally come from differing parishes and traditions. The participation is likely to be enhanced if the musicians familiarize the congregation with the music by using it as a prelude or by using preludes based on it. Instrumentalists or choristers may make other musical offerings.

Entrance hymn, psalm, or anthem. Suitable hymns for the entrance are:

219 Lord, pour thy Spirit from on high
220 God of the prophets, bless the prophets' sons
268 I bind unto myself today
H-208 Holy Spirit, ever living

A strong general hymn of praise is also suitable.

279 Praise to the Lord, the Almighty, the King of creation
280 God, my King, thy might confessing
282 Praise, my soul, the King of heaven
285 The God of Abraham praise
287 Give praise and glory unto God
786 Rejoice, ye pure in heart
H-187 All creatures of our God and King
H-190 All glory be to God on high
H-220 New songs of celebration render
H-222 O God, we praise thee, and confess
H-228 Praise the Lord! ye heavens adore him
H-231 Sing, all creation
H-233 Sing praise to God who reigns above
H-234 Sing, ye faithful, sing with gladness
H-235 Tell out, my soul
H-243 To God with gladness sing

Opening Acclamation and Collect for Purity. For the music for the Opening Acclamation, see HEAE or MMC; a common collect tone may be used for the Collect for Purity.

Litany. For music, see MMC II. A common collect tone may be used for the concluding Collect.

Ministry of the Word. Three lessons are required. A Gradual is provided after the Old Testament Lesson, and an Alleluia, Tract, or Sequence may be used after the New Testament Lesson (See GPAVT). At the Ordination of a Priest or Deacon, the Nicene Creed may be sung.

Hymn, Veni Creator Spiritus, or Veni Sancte Spiritus. For translations of Veni Creator Spiritus, see:

108 O come, Creator Spirit, come
217 Come, Holy Ghost, our souls inspire
218 Come, Holy Ghost, Creator blest
371 Creator Spirit, by whose aid
H-146 Come down, O Spirit, Love Divine
H-153, 154 O Holy Spirit, by whose breath

For translations of Veni Sancte Spiritus, see:

109 Come, thou Holy Spirit, come
H-150, 151 Holy Spirit, font of light

A period of silent prayer follows the hymn.

At the Vesting of a New Bishop. At the Ordination of a Bishop, the Additional Directions (BCP, p. 553) allow for instrumental music.

Peace. For music, see HEAE or MMC.

At the Eucharist. The liturgy continues with the Offertory. Suitable hymns for the Offertory or at the Communion or before or after the postcommunion prayer include:

219 Lord, pour thy Spirit from on high
220 God of the prophets, bless the prophets' sons
256 O Spirit of the living God
573 Go, labor on! spend and be spent
575 Lord, who didst send, by two and two before thee
786 Rejoice, ye pure in heart
H-208 Holy Spirit, ever living
H-249, 250 Ye servants of God

Blessing. For music, see HEAE or MMC.

Dismissal. For music, see HEAE or MMC.

At the Ordination of a Bishop. At the Ordination of a Bishop, the Additional Directions (BCP, p. 553) allow for a hymn of praise after the blessing and dismissal. Suitable hymns include Te Deum laudamus and general metrical hymns of praise.

Postlude. Ideally, the music at the exit of the clergy and people should be based on that hymn or text which best sums up the service.

Celebration of a New Ministry

Prelude. People usually come from differing parishes and traditions for a Celebration of a New Ministry. The participation is likely to be enhanced if the musicians will familiarize the congregation with the music by using it as a prelude or by using preludes based on it. Other musical offerings may be made by instrumentalists or choristers.

Entrance hymn, psalm, or anthem. Suitable hymns for use at the entrance include:

219 Lord, pour thy Spirit from on high
220 God of the prophets, bless the prophets' sons
268 I bind unto myself today
H-209 How lovely are thy dwellings fair

A strong general hymn of praise is also suitable:

279 Praise to the Lord, the Almighty, the King of creation
280 God, my King, thy might confessing
282 Praise, my soul, the King of heaven
285 The God of Abraham praise
287 Give praise and glory unto God
786 Rejoice, ye pure in heart
H-187 All creatures of our God and King
H-190 All glory be to God on high
H-220 New songs of celebration render
H-222 O God, we praise thee
H-228 Praise the Lord! ye heavens adore him

H-231 Sing, all creation
H-233 Sing praise to God who reigns above
H-234 Sing, ye faithful, sing with gladness
H-235 Tell out, my soul
H-243 To God with gladness sing

Litany. For music, see MMC II. A common collect tone may be used for the concluding Collect.

Liturgy of the Word. There is provision for a full series of readings: Old Testament Lesson, Gradual, Epistle and Gospel. It is appropriate to sing an Alleluia, Tract, or Sequence between the Epistle and the Gospel. (See GPAVT.)

Hymn. The sermon (and any response to it) is followed by a hymn during which representatives of the congregation and clergy process or move forward with the symbols of office to be presented. Appropriate hymns include:

219 Lord, pour thy Spirit from on high
220 God of the prophets, bless the prophets' sons
256 O Spirit of the living God
H-208 Holy Spirit, ever living
H-249, 250 Ye servants of God

Peace. For music, see HEAE or MMC.

At the Eucharist. The liturgy continues with the Offertory. Suitable hymns for use at the Offertory or at the Communion or before or after the postcommunion prayer include:

219 Lord, pour thy Spirit from on high
220 God of the prophets, bless the prophets' sons
256 O Spirit of the living God
573 Go, labor on! spend and be spent
575 Lord, who didst send, by two and two before thee
786 Rejoice, ye pure in heart
H-208 Holy Spirit, ever living
H-249, 250 Ye servants of God

Blessing and Dismissal. For music, see HEAE or MMC

Postlude. Ideally, the music at the exit of the clergy and people should be based on that hymn or text which best sums up the service.

Dedication and Consecration of a Church

Pre-service music. A bell or other musical instrument might call the people to silence for the bishop's opening words. Brass, strings, or other portable musical instruments which could later accompany the procession might perform a brief, informal prelude to the rite.

Prayer. A common collect tone may be used for the initial prayer.

Procession. Especially appropriate are hymns with an easily memorized congregational refrain, or responsorial psalms. Fitting psalms include 48, 84, 95, 100, and 118 (See GPAVT).

Opening of the Doors and Marking of the Threshold. These forms may be monotoned.

Entrance psalm. Psalm 122 and/or one of the psalms listed above may be sung responsorially as the procession comes into the church. Hymns and anthems may also be sung. Appropriate hymns include:

227 All things are thine; no gift have we
228 Only begotten, Word of God eternal
370 Spirit divine, attend our prayers
383 Blessed city, heavenly Salem
384 Christ is made the sure foundation
385 Glorious things of thee are spoken
388 I love thy kingdom, Lord
780 Christ is made the sure foundation
H-209 How lovely are thy dwellings fair

Prayer for the Consecration of the Church. This may be sung.

Processional psalm, hymn, or instrumental music. As the procession moves to the font, selected verses of Psalm 42, Canticle 9, or a hymn such as 450, THE HYMNAL 1940, "As pants the hart for cooling streams," may be sung. Also appropriate are:

H-164 All who believe and are baptized
H-165 Spirit of God, unleashed on earth

H-166 Descend, O Spirit, purging flame
H-167 O Holy Spirit, enter in
H-168 Praise and thanksgiving be to our creator
H-169 Sing praise to our creator
H-170 We know that Christ is raised
H-171 This is the Spirit's entry now

Dedication of the font. The dedication form may be sung. For the music for the Thanksgiving over the Water, see HEAE.

Processional psalm, hymn, or instrumental music. As the procession moves to the lectern-pulpit, selected verses of a psalm, hymn or instrumental music may be used, but not the organ or other instrument to be dedicated. Appropriate psalms include 25, 111, 119:1-16, and 119:89-112. Appropriate hymns include:

400 Lamp of our feet, whereby we trace
402 O Word of God incarnate
564, 785 How firm a foundation, ye saints of the Lord
H-214 Lord be thy word my rule
H-229 Praise we now the Word of grace

Dedication of the lectern and/or pulpit. This form may be sung.

Liturgy of the Word. Provision is made for an Old Testament Lesson, a Gradual, and an Epistle to be said or sung (see GPAVT).

Processional psalm, hymn, or instrumental music. As the procession moves to an appropriate place, selected verses of a psalm or hymn, or instrumental music may be used. Suitable psalms are 92, 98, and 150. Fitting hymns are 279, THE HYMNAL 1940, "Praise to the Lord, the Almighty, the King of creation" and:

H-220 New songs of celebration render
H-234 Sing, ye faithful, sing with gladness

Dedication of an instrument of music. This form may be sung. "Instrumental music may now be played, or a hymn or anthem sung." A brief fanfare would be in order, or a strong hymn of praise such as 279, THE HYMNAL 1940, "Praise to the Lord, the Almighty, the King of creation" or H-220, H-234, HYMNS III (See above).

Nicene Creed. The Nicene Creed may be sung or said if the Apostles' Creed has not already been said (that is, at a Baptism or Confirmation within the rite).

Prayers of the People. Music is provided in HEAE or MMC for Forms I and V. A common collect tone may be used for the concluding Collects.

Dedication of the Altar. This form may be sung.

Bells or instrumental music. Joyous music is suitable at the vesting of the altar.

Peace. For music, see HEAE or MMC.

At the Eucharist. The liturgy continues with the Offertory. Suitable hymns for use at the Offertory or at the Communion or before or after the postcommunion prayer include:

228 Only begotten, Word of God eternal
383 Blessed city, heavenly Salem
384 Christ is made the sure foundation
385 Glorious things of thee are spoken
388 I love thy kingdom, Lord
780 Christ is made the sure foundation
H-209 How lovely are thy dwellings fair

Blessing and Dismissal. For music, see HEAE or MMC.

Postlude. Ideally, the music at the exit of the clergy and people should be based on that hymn or text which best sums up the service.

APPENDIX I:

The Book of Canticles

A rich collection of Liturgical Music for the Holy Eucharist and for the Offices

(JAMES H. LITTON)

The recent publication of THE BOOK OF CANTICLES provides a large and diverse collection of musical settings of liturgical texts from the new BOOK OF COMMON PRAYER. With a careful study of the collection's contents, and after a new look at various rubrics in the new BOOK OF COMMON PRAYER, one should be able to consider this publication a book of musical settings which can be used to great advantage in a celebration of the Holy Eucharist as well as in the Daily Offices.

The rubric which provides for some other "song of praise" to be sung in place of the Gloria in excelsis creates an opportunity to sing a canticle as this "song of praise." Liturgical scholars point out that the use of the Gloria in excelsis as a fixed hymn of praise at the beginning of the rite was a peculiarity of the Roman rite, and the Gallican and Eastern rites make use of many other canticles or hymns, often changing them with the season. Many of the canticles are especially appropriate for certain times in the Church Year, and the following list suggests how a seasonal choice of canticles can be sung in the opening part of the Eucharist, or used in place of certain Propers.

A Table of Canticles to be sung as the "Song of Praise" (in place of Gloria in Excelsis) or as entrance songs, following Readings, at the Offertory or during Communion

Advent Season

Kyrie Eleison or Trisagion is sung in place of Gloria in excelsis. The following canticles may be sung as entrance songs, in place of the Sequence, at the Offertory, or during the Communion of the People.

Canticle 3	*or*	15	The Song of Mary, *Magnificat*: C-61—67 *or* C-132—141 (especially appropriate on the Fourth Sunday of Advent)
Canticle 4	*or*	16	The Song of Zechariah, *Benedictus Dominus Deus*: C-68—75 and C-142—150 (especially appropriate on the Second and Third Sundays of Advent)
Canticle 11			The Third Song of Isaiah, *Surge, illuminare*: C-106—115

Christmas Season

Canticle 6	*or*	20	Glory be to God *or* Glory to God, *Gloria in excelsis*: C-81—83 *or* C-170—172
Canticle 3	*or*	15	The Song of Mary, *Magnificat*: C-61—67 *or* C-132—141

Epiphany Season

Canticle 11	The Third Song of Isaiah, *Surge, illuminare*: C-106—115
Canticle 19	The Song of the Redeemed, *Magna et mirabilia*: C-164—169
Canticle 10	The Second Song of Isaiah, *Quaerite Dominum*: C-102—105
Canticle 9	The First Song of Isaiah, *Ecce, Deus*: C-96—101
Canticle 4 *or* 16	The Song of Zechariah, *Benedictus, Dominus Deus*: C-68—75 *or* C-142—150
Canticle 5 *or* 17	The Song of Simeon, *Nunc dimittis*: C-76—80 *or* C-151—157 (especially appropriate on The Feast of the Presentation of Christ in the Temple and during the last part of the Epiphany Season. Because of the text of the first verse, some may find this canticle more appropriately sung following a Reading, rather than as a hymn of praise in the first part of the Eucharist.)

Lenten Season

Kyrie Eleison or Trisagion is sung in place of Gloria in excelsis. The following canticles may be sung as entrance songs, in place of the Sequence, at the Offertory, or during the Communion of the People.

Canticle 14	A Song of Penitence, *Kyrie Pantokrator*: C-125—131
Canticle 10	The Second Song of Isaiah, *Quaerite Dominum*: C-102—105

Easter Season

Invitatory	Christ our Passover, *Pascha nostrum*: C-21—24 *or* C-43—46
Canticle 7 *or* 21	We Praise Thee *or* You are God, *Te Deum laudamus*: C-84—88 *or* C-173—177
Canticle 8	The Song of Moses, *Cantemus Domino*: C-89—95
Canticle 18	A Song to the Lamb, *Dignus es*: C-158—163

The Day of Pentecost

Canticle 7 *or* 21	We Praise Thee *or* You are God, *Te Deum laudamus*: C-84—88 *or* C-173—177
Canticle 1 *or* 12	A Song of Creation, *Benedicite, omnia opera Domini*: C-53—55 *or* C-116—118
Canticle 19	The Song of the Redeemed, *Magna et mirabilia*: C-164—169

Trinity Sunday

Canticle 7 *or* 21	We Praise Thee *or* You are God, *Te Deum laudamus*: C-84—88 *or* C-173—177
Canticle 2 *or* 13	A Song of Praise, *Benedictus es, Domini*: C-56—60 *or* C-119—124 (in place of Psalm)

General

Canticle 7 *or* 21	We Praise Thee *or* You are God, *Te Deum laudamus*: C-84—88 *or* C-173—177

Canticle 1 *or* 12	A Song of Creation, *Benedicite, omnia opera Domini*: C-53—55 *or* C-116—118
Canticle 2 *or* 13	A Song of Praise, *Benedictus es, Domini*: C-56—60 *or* C-119—124
Canticle 9	The First Song of Isaiah, *Ecce, Deus*: C-96—101
Canticle 10	The Second Song of Isaiah, *Quaerite Dominum*: C-102—105
Canticle 19	The Song of the Redeemed, *Magna et mirabilia*: C-164—169
Invitatory	Jubilate (Psalm 100): C-16—20 *or* C-37—42

Other Services

Easter Vigil

Canticle 8	The Song of Moses, *Cantemus Domino*: C-89—95 (Follows 'Israel's deliverance at the Red Sea' Lesson)
Canticle 9	The First Song of Isaiah, *Ecce, Deus*: C-96—101 (Follows 'Salvation offered freely to all' Lesson or may follow 'A new heart and a new spirit' Lesson) (Other canticles may be chosen to be sung in place of psalms following lessons in the Liturgy of the Word.)

One of the following settings may be sung at the Easter Vigil Eucharist:

Canticle 6 *or* 20	Glory be to God *or* Glory to God, *Gloria in excelsis*: C-81—83 *or* C-170—172
Canticle 7 *or* 21	We Praise Thee *or* You are God, *Te Deum laudamus*: C-84—88 *or* C-173—177

Invitatory	Christ our Passover, *Pascha nostrum*: C-21—24 *or* C-43—46

Pentecost Vigil

Canticle 2 *or* 13	A Song of Praise, *Benedictus es, Domini*: C-56—60 *or* C-119—124
Canticle 9	The First Song of Isaiah, *Ecce, Deus*: C-96—101

Third Sunday of Advent (Year B)

Canticle 3 *or* 15	The Song of Mary, *Magnificat*: C-61—67 *or* C-132—141 (in place of Psalm)

Third Sunday of Advent (Year C)

Canticle 9	The First Song of Isaiah, *Ecce, Deus*: C-96—101 (in place of Psalm)

The Annunication

Canticle 3 *or* 15	The Song of Mary, *Magnificat*: C-61—67 *or* C-132—141 (in place of Psalm)

The Visitation

Canticle 9	The First Song of Isaiah, *Ecce Deus*: C-96—101 (in place of Psalm)

The Feast of the Virgin Mary

Canticle 3 *or* 15	The Song of Mary, *Magnificat*: C-61—67 *or* C-132—141

All Major Saints' Days

Canticle 7 *or* 21	We Praise Thee *or* You are God, *Te Deum laudamus*: C-84—88 *or* C-173—177

Of the Reign of Christ

Canticle 18	A Song to the Lamb, *Dignus es*: C-158 — 163 (in place of Psalm)

Rogation Days

Canticle 1 *or* 12	A Song of Creation, *Benedicite, omnia opera Domini*: C-53—55 *or* C-116—118

Baptism

Canticle 9	The First Song of Isaiah, *Ecce, Deus*: C-96—101 (During the procession to the font as an alternative to Psalm 42.)
Canticle 19	The Song of the Redeemed, *Magna et mirabilia*: C-164—169 (During the procession from the font as an alternative to Psalm 23.)

The *Gloria in excelsis*, or some other hymn of praise (such as Canticle 9 *or* 19), may be sung in the Service of Holy Baptism immediately after the opening versicles (see BCP, p. 312).

Requiem Eucharist (at the end of the service)

Canticle 4 *or* 16	The Song of Zechariah, *Benedictus, Dominus Deus*: C-68—75 *or* C-142—150
Canticle 5 *or* 17	The Song of Simeon, *Nunc dimittis*: C-76—80 *or* C-151—157
Invitatory	Christ our Passover, *Pascha nostrum*: C-21—24 *or* C-43—46

The settings of the Gloria in excelsis (C-81—83 *or* C-170—172) in THE BOOK OF CANTICLES may, of course, be used in a Eucharist along with other settings of Eucharistic music for the Sanctus, etc.

Invitatory Psalms (Venite and Jubilate) could be used as an Introit (Entrance Song) or sung in procession instead of an opening hymn, or they might be sung as psalms of praise in place of the Gloria in excelsis. Invitatory Psalms and hymns, as well as canticles, would be sung at Morning or Evening Prayer when these Offices are used as the Service of the Word in a celebration of the Eucharist. An Order of Worship for the Evening may, of course, be used as an entrance rite for an evening celebration of the Eucharist, and the music for this order of service (C-27) along with the ancient evening hymn, Phos hilaron (C-47—52) can be found in THE BOOK OF CANTICLES.

Some parishes may find it desirable to sing the complete Pascha nostrum (C-21—24 *or* C-43—46) as a Fraction Anthem. Finally there will be many occasions when it would be appropriate to sing various Canticles with or in place of the Alleluia Verse, or in place of the Sequence, at the Offertory and during the Communion of the People. In addition to these several suggestions as to how Invitatory Psalms and Canticles may be sung in the Holy Eucharist, many parishes, no doubt, will discover other creative ways to sing these invitatories and canticles in their worship.

THE BOOK OF CANTICLES is a major contribution to the growing repertoire of music for the new BOOK OF COMMON PRAYER. Not only will it be welcomed by those who sing the Morning and Evening Offices, but it also can prove to be a rich collection of music for the Eucharist.

APPENDIX II:

Check Lists for Planning Services

Daily Morning Prayer

Date and time: ______________________

Officiant: ______________________

Prelude: ______________________

Opening Sentence (yes or no): ______ Which? ______ Sung or said: ______

Confession of Sin (yes or no): ______________________

Opening Preces (sung or said): ______________ Alleluia (yes or no): ______

Antiphon: ______________________

Before Invitatory Psalm? ______________ After Psalm? ______________

After each verse or section? ______________________

Invitatory Psalm (Venite or Jubilate) ______ *or* Christ our Passover ______

Psalm(s): ______________________ Sung or said: ______

Old Testament Lesson: ______________________

Reader: ______________________

Silence (yes or no): ______________________

Canticle: ______________________

New Testament Lesson: ______________________

Reader: ______________________

Silence (yes or no): ______________________

Sermon: ______________________

Preacher: ______________________

Canticle: ______________________

(Continued)

* Gospel Lesson: ______________________________

Reader: ______________________________

* Sermon: ______________________________

Preacher: ______________________________

Apostles' Creed: ______________________ Sung or said: ________

The Lord's Prayer and the Suffrages: ______________ Sung or said: ________

The Collect(s): ______________________ Sung or said: ________

Prayer for mission: ______________________ Sung or said: ________

Hymn or anthem: ______________________________

Special intercessions: ______________________ Sung or said: ________

Special thanksgivings: ______________________ Sung or said: ________

The General Thanksgiving (yes or no): ______________ Sung or said: ________

A Prayer of St. Chrysostom (yes or no): ______________ Sung or said: ________

Benedicamus (yes or no): ______________________ Sung or said: ________

The Grace (yes or no): __________ Which? __________ Sung or said: ________

Postlude: ______________________________

**If three Lessons are used, Gospel and sermon come in this position.*

Morning or Evening Prayer with the Holy Communion

Day or Occasion: ____________ Morning or Evening Prayer: __________

Officiant: ______________________________

Prelude: ______________________________

Opening Sentence (yes or no): _____ Which? __________ Sung or said: ________

Confession of Sin (yes or no): ______________________________

Opening Preces (sung or said): ______________ Alleluia (yes or no): ________

Antiphon: ______________________________

Before Invitatory Psalm? ______________ After Psalm? ________

After each verse or section? ______________________________

Invitatory Psalm (Venite or Jubilate) ________ *or* Christ our Passover ________

or Phos hilaron: ______________________________

Psalm(s): ______________________________ Sung or said: ________

Old Testament Lesson: ______________________________

Reader: ______________________________

Silence (yes or no): ______________________________

Canticle: ______________________________

New Testament Lesson: ______________________________

Reader: ______________________________

Silence (yes or no): ______________________________

Canticle: ______________________________

(Continued)

Gospel Lesson: ______________________________

Reader: ______________________________

Sermon: ______________________________

Preacher: ______________________________

Creed (yes or no): ____ Apostles' ____, *or* Nicene: ____ Sung or said: ____

Salutation (sung or said): ______________________________

Collect of the Day: ____________________ Sung or said: ________

Hymn or Anthem: ______________________________

Prayers of the People (sung or said): ______________________________

Leader: ______________________________

Prayer for the Whole State of Christ's Church and the World: ____________

Form I ____ ; Form II ____ ; Form III ____ ; Form IV ____ ; Form V ____ ;

Form VI ____

Other forms: The Solemn Collects, page 277: ____________

Litany for Ordinations (Ember Days), page 548: ____________

Litany of Thanksgiving (Thanksgiving Day), page 836: ____________

Litany of Thanksgiving for a Church (Dedication festival), page 578: ______

Prayers and Thanksgivings, pages 809-841, selected in conformity to directions on page 383: ______________________________

A form written for the occasion or gleaned from another source: ________

Special petitions to be included: ______________________________

Collect after the Intercessions: ____________________ Sung or said: ________

Special rites: Thanksgiving for Birth or Adoption of a Child ____ ; Commitment to Christian Service ____ ; Anointing of the Sick ____ ; Other: ________

The Peace (any special instructions): ______________________________

The Holy Communion

Offertory Sentence (yes or no): ________ Which: ________________________________

Hymn, psalm, or anthem: ____

Presenters: ____

Preparation of the Table (deacon ________ *or* assisting priest ________)

The Great Thanksgiving: ______________________ Sung or said: ________

Proper Preface: ____

Sanctus: ____

Memorial Acclamation (A, B, or D): ________________________________

Special Intercessions (D): ______________________________________

Commemoration of a Saint (B or D): ________________________________

The Lord's Prayer: ____

Fraction Anthem (yes or no): ___ Which: ____________ Alleluia (yes or no): ___

Rite One only—Prayer of Humble Access (yes or no): ________ By priest ________

or by priest and people: ____

Invitation to Communion (longer or shorter form): ________ Sung or said: ______

Ministers of Communion: ____

Hymn, psalm, or anthem during Communion: ____________________________

Hymn during Ablutions: ____

Postcommunion Prayer: ____

Hymn: ____

Blessing: ____________ Which form: ______________ Sung or said: ________

Dismissal: ____________ Alleluia (yes or no): ____________ Sung or said: ________

Deacon: ____

Postlude: ____

An Order of Service for Noonday

Date and time: ______________________________

Officiant: ______________________________

Prelude: ______________________________

Opening Preces (sung or said): ______________ Alleluia (yes or no): ________

Hymn: ______________________________

Psalm(s): ______________________________ Sung or said: ________

Scripture: ______________________________

Reader: ______________________________

Meditation: ______________________________

Leader: ______________________________

Prayers: ______________________________ Sung or said: ________

Dismissal (sung or said): ______________________________

Postlude: ______________________________

An Order of Worship for the Evening

Date and time: ______________________________

Officiant: ______________________________

Opening Acclamation: ____________________ Sung or said: ________

Lesson of Scripture (yes or no): ________ Which? ________ Sung or said: ________

Reader: ______________________________

Prayer for Light: ____________________ Sung or said: ________

Anthem, psalm, or silence: ______________________________

Phos hilaron: ______________________________

Psalm(s): ____________________ Sung or said: ________

Silence (yes or no): ______________________________

Psalter Collect (yes or no): ________________ Which? ________________

Lesson: ______________________________

Reader: ______________________________

Sermon, homily, passage from Christian literature, or silence: ________________

Preacher: ______________________________

Canticle or hymn of praise: ______________________________

Prayers: ____________________ Sung or said: ________

The Lord's Prayer: ____________________ Sung or said: ________

Concluding Collect: ____________________ Sung or said: ________

Hymn: ______________________________

Blessing: ____________________ Sung or said: ________

Dismissal: ____________ Alleluia? ____________ Sung or said: ________

Postlude: ______________________________

Daily Evening Prayer

Date and time: ______________________________

Officiant: ______________________________

Prelude: ______________________________

Opening Sentence (yes or no): ________ Which? ________ Sung or said: ________

Confession of Sin (yes or no): ______________________________

Opening Preces (sung or said): ______________ Alleluia (yes or no): ________

Phos hilaron, hymn, or Invitatory Psalm: ______________________________

Psalm(s): ______________________________ Sung or said: ________

Lesson: ______________________________

Reader: ______________________________

Silence (yes or no): ______________________________

Sermon: ______________________________

Preacher: ______________________________

Canticle: ______________________________

Apostles' Creed: ______________________________ Sung or said: ________

The Lord's Prayer and the Suffrages: ______________ Sung or said: ________

The Collect(s): ______________________________ Sung or said: ________

Prayer for mission: ______________________________ Sung or said: ________

Hymn or anthem: ______________________________

Special intercessions: ______________________________ Sung or said: ________

Special thanksgivings: ______________________________ Sung or said: ________

The General Thanksgiving (yes or no): ______________________________

A Prayer of St. Chrysostom (yes or no): ______________ Sung or said: ________

Benedicamus (yes or no): ______________________________ Sung or said: __________

The Grace (yes or no): _____________ Which? ___________ Sung or said: __________

Postlude: ____

An Order for Compline

Date and time: ________________________________

Officiant: ________________________________

Prelude: ________________________________

Opening Preces (sung or said): ________________________________

Confession of Sin (yes or no): ________________________________

Preces (sung or said): ________________ Alleluia (yes or no): ________

Psalm(s): ________________________ Sung or said: ________

Scripture: ________________________________

Reader: ________________________________

Hymn: ________________________________

The Suffrages and The Lord's Prayer (sung or said): ________________

Collects: ________________________ Sung or said: ________

Prayers: ________________________________

Antiphon: ________________ Alleluias (yes or no): ________

Nunc dimittis: ________________________________

Benedicamus and Blessing (sung or said): ________________

Postlude: ________________________________

Ash Wednesday

Celebrant: ______________________________

The silent entrance of the ministers: ______________________________

Salutation and Collect of the Day (sung or said): ______________________________

Old Testment Lesson: Joel 2:1-2, 12-17 __________ *or* Isaiah 58:1-12 __________

Reader: ______________________________

Silence (yes or no): ______________________________

Gradual: Psalm 103 __________ *or* Psalm 103:8-14 __________

Cantor: ______________________________

New Testament Lesson: 2 Corinthians 5:20b-6:10 ______________________________

Reader: ______________________________

Silence (yes or no): ______________________________

Tract and/or Sequence: ______________________________

Gospel: Matthew 6:1-6, 16-21 ______________________________

Reader: ______________________________

Sermon: ______________________________

Preacher: ______________________________

Exhortation: ______________________________

Prayer over the ashes (yes or no): __________ Sung or said: __________

Distributors of the ashes: ______________________________

Psalm 51: ______________________________

Litany of Penitence (sung or said): ______________________________

(Continued)

The Peace (any special instructions): ______________________

Offertory Sentence (yes or no): ________ Which? ______________

Hymn, psalm, or anthem: ______________________

Presenters: ______________________

Preparation of the Table (deacon ________ *or* assisting priest ________)

The Great Thanksgiving: ______________ Sung or said: ________

Proper Preface: ______________________

Sanctus: ______________________

Memorial Acclamation: ______________________

The Lord's Prayer: ______________________

Breaking of the Bread — Fraction Anthem (yes or no): ______ Which? ________

Invitation to Communion: ________ Longer or shorter form: ________

Sung or said: ______________________

Ministers of Communion: ______________________

Hymn, psalm, or anthem during Communion: ______________

Hymn during ablutions: ______________________

Postcommunion Prayer: ______________________

Hymn: ______________________

Blessing or Prayer over the People: ______________ Sung or said: ________

Dismissal: ______________________ Sung or said: ________

Deacon: ______________________

Postlude: ______________________

Palm Sunday

Celebrant: ____________________

Pre-service music: ____________________

Opening anthem: sung by choir ____ ; said ____ or sung ____ as versicle and response; said ____ or sung ____ by celebrant or cantor alone ________

Collect (sung or said): ____________________

Lesson: *Year A* Matthew 21:1-11 ______ ; *Year B* Mark 11:1-11a ______ ; *Year C* Luke 19:29-40 ____________________

Reader: ____________________

Blessing of the Palms (sung or said): ____________________

Anthem: sung by choir ____ ; said ____ or sung ____ as versicle and response; said ____ or sung ____ by celebrant or cantor alone ________

The Procession: "Let us go forth..." (sung or said): ____________

Deacon: ____________________

Hymns, psalms, or anthems: ____________________

Station Collect (yes or no): ______________ Sung or said: ________

Entry into the church: ____________________

Salutation and Collect (sung or said): ____________________

Old Testament Lesson: Isaiah 45:21-25 ______ *or* Isaiah 52:13-53:12 ______

Reader: ____________________

Silence (yes or no): ____________________

(Continued)

Gradual: Psalm 22:1-21 ______________ *or* Psalm 221:1-11 ______________

Cantor: ______________

New Testament Lesson: Philippians 2:5-11 ______________

Reader: ______________

Silence (yes or no): ______________

Tract and/or Sequence: ______________

Gospel: *Year A* Matthew 26:36-27:54 (55-66) ______ *or* 27:1-54 (55-66) ______

Year B Mark 14:32-15:39 (40-47) ______ *or* 15:1-39 (40-47) ______

Year C Luke 22:39-23:49 (50-56) ______ *or* 23:1-49 (50-56) ______

Readers or singers: ______________

Congregation standing or seated: ______________

Sermon: ______________

Preacher: ______________

Nicene Creed (yes or no): ______________

Prayers of the People: ______________ Sung or said: ______

Leader: ______________

Concluding Collect: ______________ Sung or said: ______

The Peace (any special instructions): ______________

Offertory Sentence (yes or no): ______________ Which? ______________

Hymn, psalm, or anthem: ______________

Presenters: ______________

Preparation of the Table (deacon ______ *or* assisting priest ______)

The Great Thanksgiving: ______________ Sung or said: ______

Proper Preface: ______________

Sanctus: ______________

Memorial Acclamation: ______________________________

The Lord's Prayer: ______________________________

Breaking of the Bread — Fraction Anthem (yes or no): _____ Which? __________

Invitation to Communion: _______ Longer or shorter form: __________

Sung or said: ______________________________

Ministers of Communion: __________ __________ __________

Hymn, psalm, or anthem during Communion: ______________________________

Hymn during ablutions: ______________________________

Postcommunion Prayer: ______________________________

Hymn: ______________________________

Blessing or Prayer over the People: __________ Sung or said: _______

Dismissal: ______________________________ Sung or said: _______

Deacon: ______________________________

Postlude: ______________________________

Maundy Thursday

Celebrant: ______

Prelude: ______

Entrance hymn, psalm, or anthem: ______

Opening Acclamation: ______ Sung or said: ______

Collect for Purity (yes or no): ______ Sung or said: ______

Kyrie ______ Trisagion ______ *or* Song of Praise: ______

Salutation and Collect (sung or said): ______

Old Testament Lesson: Exodus 12:1-14a ______

Reader: ______

Silence (yes or no): ______

Gradual: Psalm 78:14-20, 23-24 ______

Cantor: ______

Epistle: I Corinthians 11:23-26 (27-32) ______

Reader: ______

Silence (yes or no): ______

Tract and/or Sequence: ______

Gospel: John 13:1-15 ______ *or* Luke 22:14-30 ______

Reader: ______

Sermon: ______

Preacher: ______

Washing of Feet: ______

Anthems: ______

Prayers of the People: ______ Sung or said: ______

Leader: ____________________

Concluding Collect: ____________________ Sung or said: ________

The Peace (any special instructions): ____________________

Offertory Sentence (yes or no): ________ Which? ____________________

Hymn, psalm, or anthem: ____________________

Presenters: ____________________

Preparation of the Table (deacon ________ *or* assisting priest ________)

The Great Thanksgiving: ____________________ Sung or said: ________

Proper Preface: ____________________

Sanctus: ____________________

Memorial Acclamation: ____________________

The Lord's Prayer: ____________________

Breaking of the Bread—Fraction Anthem (yes or no): ________ Which? ________

Invitation to Communion: ________ Longer or shorter form ________

Sung or said: ____________________

Ministers of Communion: ____________________

Hymn, psalm, or anthem during Communion: ____________________

Hymn during ablutions: ____________________

Postcommunion Prayer: ____________________

Hymn: ____________________ Procession (yes or no): ________

Stripping of the altar (yes or no): ________ Psalm 22: ____________________

Blessing or Prayer over the People: ____________________ Sung or said: ________

Dismissal: ____________________ Sung or said: ________

Deacon: ____________________

Postlude: ____________________ Yes or No: ________

Good Friday

Celebrant: ____________________

The silent entrance of the ministers: ____________________

Period of silent prayer: ____________________

Salutation and Collect of the Day (sung or said): ____________________

Old Testament Lesson: Isaiah 52:13-53:12 ______ *or* Genesis 22:1-18 ______

or Wisdom 2:1, 12-24 ____________________

Reader: ____________________

Silence (yes or no): ____________________

Gradual: Psalm 22:1-11 (12-21) ______ *or* 40:1-12 ______ *or* 69:1-23 ______

Cantor ____________________

Epistle: Hebrews 10:1-25 ____________________

Reader: ____________________

Silence (yes or no): ____________________

Tract and/or Sequence: ____________________

Gospel: John 18:1—19:37 ____________ *or* 19:1-37 ____________

Readers or singers: ____________________

Congregation standing or seated: ____________________

Sermon: ____________________

Preacher: ____________________

Hymn: ____________________

The Solemn Collects: ______________________ Sung or said: ________

Deacon or other leader: ______________________

Congregation standing or kneeling, or standing for biddings and kneeling for periods of silence: ______________________

Bringing in of the Cross: ______________________

Anthems and/or hymns: ______________________

____

Preparation of the Table and bringing in of the Sacrament: ______________________

____

A Confession of Sin (Rite One or Rite Two): ______________________

The Lord's Prayer: ______________________

The Communion: ______________________

Ministers of Communion: ______________________

Concluding Prayer (p. 282), sung or said: ______________________

Holy Saturday

Celebrant: ______________________________

The silent entrance of the ministers: ______________________________

Collect of the Day (sung or said): ______________________________

Old Testament Lesson: Job 14:1-14 ______________________________

Reader: ______________________________

Silence (yes or no): ______________________________

Gradual: Psalm 130 ______________ *or* 31:1-5 ______________

Cantor: ______________________________

Epistle: I Peter 4:1-8 ______________________________

Reader: ______________________________

Silence (yes or no): ______________________________

Tract and/or Sequence: ______________________________

Gospel: Matthew 27:57-66 ______________ *or* John 19:38-42 ______________

Reader: ______________________________

Sermon: ______________________________

Preacher: ______________________________

Anthem, "In the midst of life" (BCP, pp. 484 or 492), sung or said: ______________

The Lord's Prayer: ______________________________

The Grace (BCP, page 59 or 102): ______________________________

The Great Vigil of Easter

Celebrant: ______________________________

Lighting of the Paschal Candle – Opening Address: ______________________________

Prayer (sung or said): ______________________________

"The Light of Christ . . ." (sung or said): ______________________________

The Exsultet (sung or said): ______________________________

Deacon or other person appointed: ______________________________

The Liturgy of the Word — Initial address: ______________________________

The story of Creation: Genesis 1:1-2:2: ______________________________

Reader: ______________________________

Psalm 33:1-11 ______________ *or* 36:5-10: ______________

Cantor: ______________________________

Collect: ______________________________ Sung or said: __________

The Flood: Genesis 7:1-5, 11-18; 8:6-18; 9:8-13: ______________________________

Reader: ______________________________

Psalm 46: ______________________________

Cantor: ______________________________

Collect: ______________________________ Sung or said: __________

Abraham's sacrifice of Isaac: Genesis 22:1-18: ______________________________

Reader: ______________________________

Psalm 33:12-22 ______________ *or* 16: ______________

Cantor: ______________________________

(Continued)

Collect: ______________________________ Sung or said: __________

Israel's deliverance at the Red Sea (required): Exodus 14:10-15:1: __________

Reader: ______________________________

Canticle 8, *The Song of Moses*: ______________________________

Cantor: ______________________________

Collect: ______________________________ Sung or said: __________

God's Presence in a renewed Israel: Isaiah 4:2-6: ______________________________

Reader: ______________________________

Psalm 122: ______________________________

Cantor: ______________________________

Collect: ______________________________ Sung or said: __________

Salvation offered freely to all: Isaiah 55:1-11: ______________________________

Reader: ______________________________

Canticle 9, *The First Song of Isaiah* __________ *or* Psalm 42:1-7: __________

Cantor: ______________________________

Collect: ______________________________ Sung or said: __________

A new heart and a new spirit: Ezekiel 36:24-28: ______________________________

Reader: ______________________________

Psalm 42:1-7 __________ *or* Canticle 9, *The First Song of Isaiah*: __________

Cantor: ______________________________

Collect: ______________________________ Sung or said: __________

The valley of dry bones: Ezekiel 37:1-14: ______________________________

Reader: ______________________________

Psalm 30 ______________________________ *or* 143: ______________________________

Cantor: ______________________________

Collect: ______________________ Sung or said: ________

The gathering of God's people: Zephaniah 3:12-20: ______________________

Reader: ______________________

Psalm 98 ______________ *or* 126: ______________

Cantor: ______________________

Collect: ______________________ Sung or said: ________

Holy Baptism — (Here or after the Gospel and homily): ______________________

Presentation and Examination and Baptismal Covenant (see p. 292 for address which precedes Baptismal Covenant): ______________________

Procession to the Font: ______________________

Prayers for the Candidates (sung or said): ______________________

Leader: ______________________

Concluding Collect (sung or said): ______________________

Thanksgiving over the Water (sung or said): ______________________

Consecration of the Chrism (yes or no): ______________ Sung or said: ________

The Baptism: ______________________

Procession: ______________________

Prayer (Sung or said): ______________________

The Signation and the Welcome: ______________________

At Confirmation, Reception, or Reaffirmation: Prayers

(Sung or said): ______________________

If there are no candidates for Baptism — The Renewal of Vows

(Here or after the Gospel and homily): ______________________

Prayer (Sung or said): ______________________

(Continued)

At the Eucharist — Opening Acclamation (yes or no): ______________________

Sung or said: ______________________

Canticle: ______________________

Salutation and Collect: ______________________ Sung or said: ________

Epistle: Romans 6:3-11 ______________________

Reader: ______________________

Silence (yes or no): ______________________

Alleluia: ______________________

Psalm 114 ______________ *or* other psalm or hymn: ______________

Gospel: Matthew 28:1-10 ______________________

Reader: ______________________

Sermon: ______________________

Preacher: ______________________

Prayers of the People: ______________________ Sung or said: ________

Leader: ______________________

Concluding Collect: ______________________ Sung or said: ________

The Peace (any special instructions): ______________________

Offertory Sentence (yes or no): ________ Which? ______________

Hymn, psalm, or anthem: ______________________

Presenters: ______________________

Preparation of the Table (deacon ________ *or* assisting priest ________)

The Great Thanksgiving: ______________________ Sung or said: ________

Proper Preface: ______________________

Sanctus: ______________________

Memorial Acclamation: ______________________

The Lord's Prayer: ______________________________

Fraction Anthem (yes or no): ____________ Which? _____ (Alleluia is used) _____

Invitation to Communion: ____________ Longer or shorter form: ______________

Sung or said: ______________________________

Ministers of Communion: ______________________________

Hymn, psalm, or anthem during Communion: ______________________

Hymn during ablutions: ______________________________

Postcommunion Prayer: ______________________________

Hymn: ______________________________

Blessing: ______________________________ Sung or said: ________

Dismissal (with "Alleluia, alleluia"): ____________________ Sung or said: ________

Deacon: ______________________________

Postlude: ______________________________

The Vigil of Pentecost

Celebrant: ______________________________

The Service of Light — Opening Acclamation: __________ Sung or said: __________

Lesson of Scripture (yes or no): ________ Which? ________ Sung or said ______

Reader: ______________________________

Prayer for Light: ______________________________ Sung or said: __________

Anthem, psalm, or silence: ______________________________

Phos hilaron or other hymn: ______________________________

At the Eucharist — Salutation and Collect: ______________ Sung or said: ________

The Tower of Babel: Genesis 11:1-9: ______________________________

Reader: ______________________________

Silence (yes or no): ______________________________

Psalm 33:12-22 ____________ *or* another psalm, canticle, or hymn: __________

Cantor: ______________________________

The Covenant at Sinai: Exodus 19:1-9, 16-20a; 20:18-20: ______________

Reader: ______________________________

Silence (yes or no): ______________________________

Canticle 2 ______ *or* 13 ______ *or* another canticle, psalm or hymn: ______

Cantor: ______________________________

The Dry Bones: Ezekiel 37:1-14: ______________________________

Reader: ______________________________

Silence (yes or no): ______________________________

Psalm 130 ____________ *or* another psalm, canticle, or hymn: __________

Cantor: ______________________________

The Outpouring of the Spirit: Joel 2:28-32: ______________________

Reader: ______________________

Silence (yes or no): ______________________

Canticle 9 __________ *or* another canticle, psalm or hymn: __________

Cantor: ______________________

Pentecost: Acts 2:1-11: ______________________

Reader: ______________________

Silence (yes or no): ______________________

Psalm 104:25-32 __________ *or* another psalm, canticle, or hymn: __________

Cantor: ______________________

The Spirit you received: Romans 8:14-17, 22-27: ______________________

Reader: ______________________

Silence (yes or no): ______________________

Alleluia and/or Sequence: ______________________

Gospel: John 7:37-39a: ______________________

Reader: ______________________

Sermon: ______________________

Preacher: ______________________

Holy Baptism ______________________

Presentation and Examination and Baptismal Covenant: __________

Procession to the Font: ______________________

Prayers for the Candidates (sung or said): __________

Leader: ______________________

(Continued)

Concluding Collect (sung or said): ______________________________

Thanksgiving over the Water (sung or said): ______________________

Consecration of the Chrism (yes or no): ___ Sung or said: __________

The Baptism: ____

Procession: ____

Prayer (sung or said): ___________________________________

The Signation and the Welcome: ___________________________

At Confirmation, Reception, or Reaffirmation: Prayers

(Sung or said): _______________________________________

The Peace (any special instructions): ______________________

If there are no candidates for Baptism — The Renewal of Vows (BCP, p. 292)

Prayer (Sung or said): ___________________________________

Prayers of the People: __________________________ Sung or said: ______

Leader: ____

Concluding Collect: ____________________________ Sung or said: ______

If there were no baptisms, the Peace (any special instructions): __________

Offertory Sentence (yes or no): ______ Which? ____________________

Hymn, psalm, or anthem: _________________________________

Presenters: ____

Preparation of the Table (deacon ______ *or* assisting priest ______)

The Great Thanksgiving: __________________________ Sung or said: ______

Proper Preface: ____

Sanctus: ____

Memorial Acclamation: ___________________________________

The Lord's Prayer: ____

Fraction Anthem (yes or no): ________ Which? ____________________

(Alleluia) ____

Invitation to Communion: ___________ Longer or shorter form: __________

Sung or said: ____

Ministers of Communion: ____

Hymn, psalm, or anthem during Communion: _________________________

Hymn during ablutions: ____

Postcommunion Prayer: ____

Hymn: ____

Blessing: ______________________________________ Sung or said: _______

Dismissal (with "Alleluia, alleluia"): _________________ Sung or said _______

Deacon: ____

Postlude: ____

Holy Baptism

Date and Time: ______________________

Celebrant: ______________________

Prelude: ______________________

Entrance hymn, psalm, or anthem: ______________________

Opening Acclamation: ______________________ Sung or said: ________

Versicles (sung or said): ______________________

Salutation and Collect: ______________________ Sung or said: ________

Old Testament Lesson: ______________________

Reader: ______________________

Silence (yes or no): ______________________

Gradual: Psalm ______________________

Cantor: ______________________

New Testament Lesson: ______________________

Reader: ______________________

Silence (yes or no): ______________________

Alleluia or Tract and/or Sequence: ______________________

Gospel Lesson: ______________________

Reader: ______________________

Sermon: ______________________

Preacher: ______________________

Presentation and Examination and Baptismal Covenant: ______________________

Procession to the Font: ______________________

Prayers for the Candidates (sung or said): ____________________

Leader: ____________________

Concluding Collect (sung or said): ____________________

Thanksgiving over the Water (sung or said): ____________________

Consecration of the Chrism (yes or no): __________ Sung or said: ______

The Baptism: ____________________

Procession: ____________________

Prayer (sung or said): ____________________

The Signation and the Welcome: ____________________

At Confirmation, Reception, or Reaffirmation: Prayers

Sung or said: ____________________

The Peace (any special instructions): ____________________

Prayers of the People: __________ Sung or said: ______

Leader: ____________________

Concluding Collect: __________ Sung or said: ______

Offertory Sentence (yes or no): ______ Which? ____________________

Hymn, psalm, or anthem: ____________________

Presenters: ____________________

Preparation of the Table (deacon ______ *or* assisting priest ______)

The Great Thanksgiving: __________ Sung or said: ______

Proper Preface: ____________________

Sanctus: ____________________

Memorial Acclamation: ____________________

(Continued)

The Lord's Prayer: ______________________________

Fraction Anthem (yes or no): ______ Which? ______ Alleluia (yes or no): ______

Invitation to Communion: ____________ Longer or shorter form: ____________

Sung or said: ______________________________

Ministers of Communion: ______________________________

Hymn, psalm, or anthem during Communion: ______________________________

Hymn during ablutions: ______________________________

Postcommunion Prayer: ______________________________

Hymn: ______________________________

Blessing (yes or no): ________ Which form: ____________ Sung or said: ______

Dismissal: __________ Alleluia (yes or no): __________ Sung or said: __________

Deacon: ______________________________

Postlude: ______________________________

The Holy Eucharist: Rite One

Day or Occasion: ______________________
Celebrant: ______________________

The Entrance Rite

Special entrance rites for certain days or occasions: ______________

Ash Wednesday, page 264 ______ Confirmation, page 413 ______

Palm Sunday, page 270 ______ Marriage, page 423 ______

Good Friday, page 276 ______ Ministration to the Sick, page 453 ______

Holy Saturday, page 283 ______ Burial of the Dead, page 469 ______

Easter Vigil, page 285 ______ Ordinations, pages 512, 525, 537 ______

Pentecost Vigil, page 227 ______ Celebration of a New Ministry, page 559 ______

Holy Baptism, page 299 ______ Consecration of a Church, page 567 ______

Option I: Normal in festal seasons, permitted except in Advent and Lent: ______

____

Prelude: ______________________

Entrance hymn, psalm, or anthem: ______________________

Opening Acclamation: ______________ Sung or said: ______

Collect for Purity (sung or said): ______________________

Decalogue ______ *or* Summary of the Law ______ *or* neither: ______

Kyrie ______ *or* Trisagion ______ (yes or no): ______ Which form? ______

Song of Praise: ______________________

(Continued)

Option II: Normal in Advent and Lent, permitted except at certain festal times: ____

____

Prelude: ______________________________

Entrance hymn, psalm, or anthem: ______________________________

Opening Acclamation: ______________ Sung or said: __________

Collect for Purity (sung or said): ______________________________

Decalogue ________ *or* Summary of the Law ________ *or* neither: ________

Kyrie ______________ *or* Trisagion ______________

Option III: A Penitential Order, page 319: ______________________________

Prelude: ______________________________

Entrance hymn, psalm, or anthem: ______________________________

Opening Acclamation: ______________ Sung or said: __________

Decalogue (yes or no): ______________________________

Sentence of Scripture: ______________________________

Kyrie __________ Trisagion __________ *or* Song of praise: __________

Option IV: The Great Litany: ______________ Sung or said: __________

Litanist: ______________________________

Option V: An Order of Worship for the Evening: ______________________________

Opening Acclamation ______________ Sung or said: __________

Lesson of Scripture (yes or no): ______ Which? ______ Sung or said: __________

Reader: ______________________________

Prayer for Light: ______________ Sung or said: __________

Anthem, psalm, or silence: ______________________________

Phos hilaron: ______________________________

The Ministry of the Word

Collect of the Day: ______________________________ Sung or said: ________

Old Testament Lesson: ______________________________

Reader: ______________________________

Silence (yes or no): ______________________________

Gradual: Psalm ______________________________

Cantor: ______________________________

New Testament Lesson: ______________________________

Reader: ______________________________

Silence (yes or no): ______________________________

Alleluia or Tract and/or Sequence: ______________________________

Gospel Lesson: ______________________________

Reader: ______________________________

Sermon: ______________________________

Preacher: ______________________________

Reaffirmation of Vows, page 292 (Easter, Pentecost, Epiphany I,

All Saints' Day or the Sunday after All Saints' Day); page 303 (Baptism);

page 416 (Confirmation): ______________________________

Nicene Creed (yes or no): ______________________________ Sung or said: ________

Prayers of the People (sung or said): ______________________________

Leader: ______________________________

Prayer for the Whole State of Christ's Church and the World: ____________

Form I ___ Form II ___ Form III ___ Form IV ___ Form V ___ Form VI ___

(Continued)

Other forms: The Solemn Collects, page 277: ______

Litany for Ordinations (Ember Days), page 548: ______

Litany of Thanksgiving (Thanksgiving Day), page 836: ______

Litany of Thanksgiving for a Church (Dedication festival), page 578: ______

A form written for the occasion or gleaned from another source: ______

______

Special petitions to be included: ______

______

Collect after the Intercessions: ______ Sung or said: ______

Confession of Sin (yes or no): ______

Bidding: ______

Confession: ______

Comfortable Words: ______

Special rites: Thanksgiving for Birth or Adoption of a Child ______

Commitment to Christian Service ______

Anointing of the Sick ______ Other ______

The Peace (any special instructions): ______

The Holy Communion

Offertory Sentence (yes or no): ______ Which? ______

Hymn, psalm, or anthem: ______

Presenters: ______

Preparation of the Table (deacon ______ *or* assisting priest ______)

The Great Thanksgiving (I or II): ____________________ Sung or said: ________

Proper Preface: ____

Sanctus: ____

Benedictus qui venit: ____

The Lord's Prayer: ____

Fraction Anthem (yes or no): ______ Which? ______ Alleuia (yes or no): ______

Prayer of Humble Access (yes or no): ______________ By priest ______________,

or by priest and people: ____

Invitation to Communion (yes or no): ___ Longer or shorter form: ___________

Sung or said: ____

Ministers of Communion: ____

Hymn, psalm, or anthem during Communion: ____________________________

Hymn during ablutions: ____

Postcommunion Prayer by priest ________ *or* by priest and people: ________

Hymn: ____

Blessing (longer or shorter form): ____________________ Sung or said: ________

Dismissal (yes or no): ______ Which form? ______ Alleluia (yes or no): ______

Sung or said: ______________________ Deacon: ______________________

Postlude: ____

The Holy Eucharist: Rite Two

Day or Occasion: ______________________________

Celebrant: ______________________________

The Entrance Rite

Special entrance rites for certain days or occasions: ______________

Ash Wednesday, page 264 ____ Confirmation, page 413 ____________

Palm Sunday, page 270 ____ Marriage, page 423 ____________

Good Friday, page 276 ____ Ministration to the Sick, page 453 ________

Holy Saturday, page 283 ____ Burial of the Dead, page 491 ________

Easter Vigil, page 285 ____ Ordinations, pages 512, 525, 537 ________

Pentecost Vigil, page 227 ____ Celebration of a New Ministry, page 559 ____

Holy Baptism, page 299 ____ Consecration of a Church, page 567 ______

Option I: Normal in festal seasons, permitted except in Advent or Lent: ______

____

Prelude: ______________________________

Entrance hymn, psalm or anthem: ______________________

Opening Acclamation: ______________ Sung or said: ______

Collect for Purity (yes or no): ____________ Sung or said: ______

Song of Praise: ______________________________

Option II: Normal in Advent and Lent, permitted except at certain festal times: ___

____

Prelude: ______________________________

Entrance hymn, psalm, or anthem: ______________________________

Opening Acclamation: ____________________ Sung or said: ________

Collect for Purity (yes or no): ______________ Sung or said: ________

Kyrie ____________________ *or* Trisagion ____________________

Option III: A Penitential Order, page 351: ______________________________

Prelude: ______________________________

Entrance hymn, psalm, or anthem: ______________________________

Opening Acclamation: ____________________ Sung or said: ________

Decalogue (yes or no): ______________________________

Sentence of Scripture: ______________________________

Kyrie eleison ________ Trisagion ________ *or* Song of praise: ________

Option IV: The Great Litany: ____________________ Sung or said: ________

Litanist: ______________________________

Option V: An Order of Worship for the Evening: ______________________

Opening Acclamation ____________________ Sung or said: ________

Lesson of Scripture (yes or no): ______ Which? ______ Sung or said: ________

Reader: ______________________________

Prayer for Light ____________________ Sung or said: ________

Anthem, psalm, or silence: ______________________________

Phos hilaron: ______________________________

(Continued)

The Ministry of the Word

Collect of the Day: ______________________________ Sung or said: ________

Old Testament Lesson: ______________________________

Reader: ______________________________

Silence (yes or no): ______________________________

Gradual: Psalm ______________________________

Cantor: ______________________________

New Testament Lesson: ______________________________

Reader: ______________________________

Silence (yes or no): ______________________________

Alleluia or Tract and/or Sequence: ______________________________

Gospel Lesson: ______________________________

Reader: ______________________________

Sermon: ______________________________

Preacher: ______________________________

Reaffirmation of Vows, page 292 (Easter, Pentecost, Epiphany I, All Saints' Day or the Sunday after All Saints' Day); page 303 (Baptism); page 416 (Confirmation) ______________________________

Nicene Creed (yes or no): ______________________________ Sung or said: ________

Prayers of the People (sung or said): ______________________________

Leader: ______________________________

Form I ____ Form II ____ Form III ____ Form IV ____ Form V ____ Form VI ____

Other forms: the Solemn Collects, page 277: ______________________________

Litany for Ordinations (Ember Days), page 548 ______________________________

Litany of Thanksgiving (Thanksgiving Day), page 836 ______________

Litany of Thanksgiving for a Church (Dedication festival), page 578 ________

A form written for the occasion or gleaned from another source: __________

____

Special petitions to be included: ______________________________

____

Collect after the Intercessions: ______________ Sung or Said: ________

Confession of Sin (yes or no): ______________________________

Special rites: Thanksgiving for Birth or Adoption of a Child ______________

Commitment to Christian Service ______________________________

Anointing of the Sick ____________ Other ______________

The Peace (any special instructions): __________________________

The Holy Communion

Offertory Sentence (yes or no): ________ Which? ______________

Hymn, psalm, or anthem: ______________________________

Presenters: ______________________________

Preparation of the Table (deacon ________ *or* assisting priest ________)

The Great Thanksgiving (A, B, C, or D): ____________ Sung or said: ________

Proper Preface: (A or B): ______________________________

Sanctus: ______________________________

Memorial Acclamation : ______________________________

Special Intercessions (D): ______________________________

Commemoration of a Saint (B or D): __________________________

(Continued)

The Lord's Prayer: ______________________________

Fraction Anthem (yes or no): ______ Which? ______ Alleluia (yes or no): ______

Invitation to Communion (longer or shorter form): ______ Sung or said: ______

Ministers of Communion: ______________________________

Hymn, psalm, or anthem during Communion: ______________________________

Hymn during ablutions: ______________________________

Postcommunion Prayer: ______________________________

Hymn: ______________________________

Blessing (yes or no): ______ Which Form? ______ Sung or said: ______

Dismissal: ______ Alleluia (yes or no): ______ Sung or said: ______

Deacon: ______________________________

Postlude: ______________________________

Confirmation, Reception, or Reaffirmation of Baptismal Vows

Date and Time: ______________________________

Celebrant: ______________________________

Prelude: ______________________________

Entrance hymn, psalm, or anthem: ______________________________

Opening Acclamation: ______________________ Sung or said: ________

Versicles: ______________________________

Salutation and Collect: ______________________ Sung or said: ________

Old Testament Lesson: ______________________________

Reader: ______________________________

Silence (yes or no): ______________________________

Gradual: Psalm ______________________________

Cantor: ______________________________

New Testament Lesson: ______________________________

Reader: ______________________________

Silence (yes or no): ______________________________

Alleluia or Tract and/or Sequence: ______________________________

Gospel Lesson: ______________________________

Reader: ______________________________

Sermon: ______________________________

Preacher: ______________________________

(Continued)

Presentation and Examination: ____________________

Prayers for the Candidates (sung or said): ____________________

Leader: ____________________

Concluding Prayer (sung or said): ____________________

The Laying on of Hands: ____________________

Prayer (sung or said): ____________________

The Peace (any special instructions): ____________________

Prayers of the People: ____________________ Sung or said: ________

Leader: ____________________

Concluding Collect: ____________________ Sung or said: ________

Offertory Sentence (yes or no): ____________________ Which? ________

Hymn, psalm, or anthem: ____________________

Presenters: ____________________

Preparation of the Table (deacon ________ *or* assisting priest ________)

The Great Thanksgiving: ____________________ Sung or said: ________

Proper Preface: ____________________

Sanctus: ____________________

Memorial Acclamation: ____________________

The Lord's Prayer: ____________________

Fraction Anthem (yes or no): ______ Which? ______ Alleluia (yes or no): ______

Invitation to Communion: ________ Longer or shorter form: ________

Sung or said: ____________________

Ministers of Communion: ____________________

Hymn, psalm, or anthem during Communion: ____________________

Hymn during ablutions: ____________________

Postcommunion Prayer: ____

Hymn: ____

Blessing (yes or no): ________ Which form: ______________ Sung or said: __________

Dismissal: ___________ Alleluia (yes or no): ___________ Sung or said: ___________

Deacon: ____

Postlude: ____

Celebration and Blessing of a Marriage

Names of the couple: ______________________________

____

Date and time of rite: ______________________________

Celebrant: ______________________________

Prelude: ______________________________

____

____

Entrance hymn, psalm, anthem, or instrumental music: ______________________________

____

Order of procession: ______________________________

____

____

Exhortation, Charge, Declaration of Consent: ______________________________

Presentation or Giving in Marriage: ______________________________

Hymn, psalm, or anthem: ______________________________

Salutation and Collect (sung or said): ______________________________

Old Testament Lesson: ______________________________

Reader: ______________________________

Silence (yes or no): ______________________________

Gradual: Psalm ______________________________

Cantor: ______________________________

New Testament Lesson: ______________________________

Reader: ______________________________

Silence (yes or no): ______________________________

Alleluia or Tract and/or Sequence: ______________________________

Gospel Lesson: ______________________________

Reader: ______________________________

Sermon: ______________________________

Preacher: ______________________________

Apostles' Creed (yes or no): ______________________________

Giving of the ring(s), single or double ring ceremony: ______________________________

Blessing of the ring(s) (yes or no): ______________________________

Form to be used with giving of the ring(s): ______________________________

The Prayers: ______________________________ Sung or said: __________

Leader: ______________________________

The Blessing: ______________________________ Sung or said: __________

The Peace (any special instructions): ______________________________

Offertory Sentence (yes or no): ________ Which? ______________________________

Hymn, psalm, anthem, or instrumental music: ______________________________

Presenters: ______________________________

Preparation of the Table (deacon __________ *or* assisting priest __________)

The Great Thanksgiving: ______________________________ Sung or said: __________

Proper Preface: ______________________________

Sanctus: ______________________________

Memorial Acclamation: ______________________________

The Lord's Prayer: ______________________________

(Continued)

Fraction Anthem (yes or no): ______ Which? ______ Alleluia (yes or no): ______

Invitation to Communion: __________ Longer or shorter form: __________

Sung or said: ______________________________

Ministers of Communion: ______________________________

Hymn, psalm, or anthem during Communion: ______________________________

Hymn during ablutions: ______________________________

Postcommunion Prayer (celebrant ______ *or* celebrant and people: ______)

Hymn: ______________________________

Blessing and/or dismissal: ______________________________

Hymn, psalm, anthem, or instrumental music: ______________________________

____

Burial of the Dead:

Name of the deceased: ____________________

Date and time of the rite: ____________________

Celebrant: ____________________

Prelude: ____________________

Opening Anthems: ____________________ Sung or said: ________

Salutation and Collect: (sung or said) ____________________

Old Testament Lesson: ____________________

Reader: ____________________

Silence (yes or no): ____________________

Gradual: Psalm ____________________

Cantor: ____________________

New Testament Lesson: ____________________

Reader: ____________________

Silence (yes or no): ____________________

Alleluia or Tract and/or Sequence: ____________________

Gospel Lesson: ____________________

Reader: ____________________

Sermon: ____________________

Preacher: ____________________

Apostles' Creed (yes or no): ____________________

The Prayers: ____________________ Sung or said: ________

Leader: ____________________

(Continued)

Concluding Collect (Rite II): ______________________ Sung or said: ________

The Peace (any special instructions): ______________________________

Offertory Sentence (yes or no): ______________________ Which? ________

Hymn, psalm, or anthem: ______________________________________

Presenters: ____

Preparation of the Table (deacon ________ *or* assisting priest ________)

The Great Thanksgiving: ______________________ Sung or said: ________

Proper Preface: ____

Sanctus: ____

Memorial Acclamation: ____________________________________

The Lord's Prayer: ____

Fraction Anthem (yes or no): ______ Which? ______ Alleluia (yes or no): ______

Invitation to Communion: __________ Longer or shorter form: __________

Sung or said: ____

Ministers of Communion: __________________________________

Hymn, psalm, or anthem during Communion: ______________________

Hymn during ablutions: ______________________________________

Postcommunion Prayer (celebrant ________ *or* celebrant and people: ________)

Anthem or hymn: ____

The Commendation (sung or said): ______________________________

Blessing and/or Dismissal: ______________________ Sung or said: ________

Hymn, anthem(s), or canticle: __________________________________

Postlude: ____

The Committal — Anthem(s): ______________________ Sung or said: ________

Prayers: ____ Sung or said: ________

Dismissal: ______________________________________ Sung or said: ________

Hymn: ____

Blessing: ______________________________ Sung or said: ______

Dismissal: ________ Alleluia (yes or no): ________ Sung or said: ________

Deacon: ____

Hymn of praise (ordination of a bishop only): ____________________

Postlude: ____

Celebration of a New Ministry

New Minister: ______________________

Date and time: ______________________

Celebrant: ______________________

Prelude: ______________________

Hymn, psalm, or anthem: ______________________

The Institution: ______________________

Presenters: ______________________

Litany for Ordinations (p. 548): __________ *or* other Litany: __________

Sung or said: ______________________

Litanist: ______________________

Salutation and Collect: ______________________ Sung or said: __________

Old Testament Lesson: ______________________

Reader: ______________________

Silence (yes or no): ______________________

Gradual: Psalm ______________________

Cantor: ______________________

New Testament Lesson: ______________________

Reader: ______________________

Silence (yes or no): ______________________

Alleluia or Tract and/or Sequence: ______________________

Gospel Lesson: ______________________

Deacon: ______________________

Sermon: ____________________

Preacher: ____________________

Response(s): ____________________

Hymn: ____________________

Induction: ____________________

Presenters of symbols —

Bible: ____________________

Stole: ____________________

Book of Prayers: ____________________

Olive oil: ____________________

Keys (a warden): ____________________

Constitution and Canons (diocesan clergy): ____________________

Bread and wine: ____________________

The Peace (any special instructions): ____________________

Offertory Sentence (yes or no): ________ Which? ____________________

Hymn, psalm, or anthem: ____________________

Presenters: ____________________

Preparation of the Table (deacon ________ *or* assisting priest ________)

The Great Thanksgiving: ____________________ Sung or said: ________

Proper Preface: ____________________

Sanctus: ____________________

Memorial Acclamation: ____________________

The Lord's Prayer: ____________________

(Continued)

Fraction Anthem (yes or no): ________ Which? ________ Alleluia (yes or no): ______

Invitation to Communion: ________ Longer or shorter form: ________

Sung or said: ________________________________

Ministers of Communion: ________________________________

Hymn, psalm, or anthem during Communion: ________________________________

Hymn during ablutions: ________________________________

Postcommunion Prayer: ________________________________

Hymn: ________________________________

Blessing: ________________________________ Sung or said: ________

Dismissal: ________ Alleluia (yes or no): ________ Sung or said: ________

Deacon: ________________________________

Postlude: ________________________________

Dedication and Consecration of a Church

Date and time: ______

Celebrant: ______

Prelude: ______

Exhortation and Prayer: ______ Sung or said: ______

Procession — hymns, psalms, anthems or instrumental music: ______

______

Opening of the doors: ______

Signing of the threshold (sung or said): ______

Psalm: ______

Hymns or anthems: ______

Prayer for the Consecration: ______ Sung or said: ______

Processional psalm, hymn, or instrumental music: ______

Dedication of the Font: ______ Sung or said: ______

Processional psalm, hymn, or instrumental music: ______

Dedication of lectern-pulpit: ______ Sung or said: ______

Old Testament Lesson: ______

Reader: ______

Silence (yes or no): ______

Gradual: Psalm ______

Cantor: ______

New Testament Lesson: ______

Reader: ______

(Continued)

Silence (yes or no): ______

Processional psalm, hymn, or instrumental music: ______

Dedication of instrument of music: ______ Sung or said: ______

Instrumental music, hymn or anthem: ______

Gospel Lesson: ______

Deacon: ______

Sermon: ______

Preacher: ______

Nicene Creed (yes or no): ______ Sung or said: ______

Prayers of the People: ______ Sung or said: ______

Deacon or leader: ______

Concluding Prayers: ______ Sung or said: ______

Dedication of the Altar: ______ Sung or said: ______

Vesting of the Altar: ______

Bells or instrumental music: ______

The Peace (any special instructions): ______

Offertory Sentence (yes or no): ______ Which? ______

Hymn, psalm, or anthem: ______

Presenters: ______

Preparation of the Table (deacon ______ *or* assisting priest ______

The Great Thanksgiving: ______ Sung or said: ______

Proper Preface: ______

Sanctus: ______

Memorial Acclamation: ______

The Lord's Prayer: ______

Fraction Anthem (yes or no): ______ Which? ______ Alleluia (yes or no): ______

Invitation to Communion: __________ Longer or shorter form: __________

Sung or said: ____________________

Ministers of Communion: ____________________

Hymn, psalm, or anthem during Communion: ____________________

Hymn during ablutions: ____________________

Postcommunion Prayer: ____________________

Hymn: ____________________

Blessing: ____________________ Sung or said: ______

Dismissal: __________ Alleluia (yes or no): __________ Sung or said: ______

Deacon: ____________________

Postlude: ____________________

APPENDIX III:

Some Available Musical Settings of Eucharistic Rite Two

(1979) (DAVID FARR and RICHARD PROULX)

This list has been compiled as a resource tool for those seeking new congregational settings of Eucharistic texts. Included are recent works readily available which appear to have wide usefulness and appeal and are well-crafted. They represent many musical styles and thus provide a resource for those contemplating the composition of additional settings. The list does not pretend to be definitive or complete — there are, no doubt, other fine settings which have not come to our attention during the process of compilation and revision. Moreover, many fine works are frequently produced in local areas, but do not have national distribution; these compositions should also be included in one's search for available material. Suitable music is where you find it — there is no single source! Musical settings vary as much as the individual circumstances which produce them: herein are works for congregation only, cantor and congregation, small or large choir and congregation, or (in a few cases) choir only.

The Rite Two text is an ecumenical product of the International Consultation on English Texts (ICET). Therefore, most parts of Roman Catholic, Episcopal, Lutheran, Methodist, and Presbyterian settings of the Eucharistic "Ordinary" are interchangeable. New services produced for the Church of England are known as "Series 3," which contain minor variations to that used by the Episcopal Church, notably (1) separation of Sanctus and Benedictus (although they can frequently be joined for American performance); (2) a different text for the Fraction Anthem, which may be used as "some other suitable anthem" (BCP, p. 364); and (3) variant texts for some of the Acclamations.

Composing music for congregational singing presents unique challenges. Such music needs to be easily learned and remembered by inexperienced singers and should express the text within a logical musical framework. However, it must also be musically interesting (even irresistible!), expressive of the depths of the human spirit and, of course, be worthy of mankind's ultimate endeavor, which worship is. Plainsong, for instance, expressed these ideals within the life of medieval monastic communities.

Today, however, the unison song of the community can be surrounded by the sonorities of other musical resources; keyboards, guitars, bells, orchestras, choirs, solo singers, electronic tape, and rhythmic instruments can all be used to great advantage in enlivening the corporate experience of parish worship. Any given text has inherent problems and opportunities which the composer must deal with, since all good vocal music carries its text well. Elements such as rhythm, syllabic accentuation, phrase length and syntactual clarity are all obvious considerations. There is also a strong pastoral aspect to the composer's ministry in that he/she will adequately challenge all performers — that is, stretch their abilities and ears — without making impossible performance demands upon them. Moreover, the clever composer will see to it that there is a suitable balance among the performing resources. Further, the rehearsal for the congregation's part can sometimes be built directly into the music itself in an artful manner, thereby eliminating distracting pre-liturgy congregational rehearsals. The skillful use of thematic motifs treated responsorially between cantor, choir, congregation and instruments is one way of creating the necessary musical inevitablility in the response of all these forces. (Some of the best settings from both former and our own times employ an economy of musical ideas, which are presented in identical patterns throughout the work. It is possible, for example, to use the same tune for the Gloria "Amen," Eucharistic Acclamation, and Great Amen, which can unify the liturgy and give added mileage to already-learned tunes.)

The thoughtful composer will create a vehicle for parish worship which wears well and remains fresh and attractive through repeated use.

This committee has examined many settings of the ICET Eucharistic texts which do not adequately represent the foregoing criteria and which therefore have not been included in this list. It is hoped that composers will continue to bring their most creative skills to the unique challenge of composing pastorally sensitive liturgical music for the Church of our present day.

Key to Abbreviations

K	*Kyrie (Lord have mercy)*
Tr	*Trisagion (Holy God . . .)*
G	*Gloria in excelsis (Glory to God)*
Cr	*Credo (Nicene Creed)*
S	*Sanctus (Holy, Holy, Holy) & Benedictus unless otherwise noted*
Ac	*Acclamations*
Am	*Great Amen*
LP	*Lord's Prayer*
AD	*Agnus Dei (Lamb of God, or Jesus, Lamb of God)*
Xp	*Christ our Passover*

Collections

Title	Publisher	Forces Required	Portions of Text Se
Church Hymnal Series I: Five Settings of the Common Texts of the Holy Eucharist	CHC	Unison	K,Tr,G,S,Ac, LP,AD,Xp
Congregational Music for Eucharist	CHC	Various	K,Tr,G,Cr,S,Ac, LP,AD,Xp
Music for Eucharist (Rite Two)	GIA (G-2060, G-2061)	Various	K,Tr,G,Cr,S,Ac, Am,LP,AD,Xp

Publishers of the Listed Works

(Agape)

Agape
380 South Main Place
Carol Stream, IL 60187

(Assoc)

Associated Music Publishers
866 Third Avenue, c/o G. Schirmer
New York, NY 10022

(Augsburg)

Augsburg Publishing House
426 South Fifth Street
Minneapolis, MN 55415

(B&H)

Boosey & Hawkes, Inc.
Oceanside
NY 11572

(Calvary)

Calvary Press
c/o Randall M. Eagan & Assoc.
2024 Kenwood Parkway
Minneapolis, MN 55405

(CHC)

The Church Hymnal Corporation
800 Second Avenue
New York, NY 10017

(Comm. St. Mary)

The Community of St. Mary
John Street
Peekskill, NY 10566

(EV)

Elkan-Vogel, Inc.
c/o Theodore Presser
Presser Place
Bryn Mawr, PA 19010

(Gem)

Gemini Press, Inc.
c/o Alexander Broude
225 West 57 Street
New York, NY 10019

(GWM)

General Words & Music Co.
c/o Neil A. Kjos Music Co.
525 Busse Highway
Park Ridge, IL 60068

(GIA)

G.I.A. Publications, Inc.
7404 South Mason Avenue
Chicago, IL 60638

(Hinshaw)

Hinshaw Music, Inc.
PO Box 470
Chapel Hill, NC 27514

(Hope)

Hope Publishing Company
380 South Main Place
Carol Stream, IL 60187

(Mayhew-McCrimmon)

Mayhew-McCrimmon, Ltd.
10-12 High Street
Great Wakering SS3 OEQ
England

(Nov)

Novello Publications, Inc.
145 Palisade Street
Dobbs Ferry, NY 10522

(OUP)

Oxford University Press
200 Madison Avenue
New York, NY 10016

(RSCM)

The Royal School of Church Music
Addington Palace
Croydon, CR9 5AD
England

(St. Mary's Press)

St. Mary's Press
Wantage, Oxon. OX12 9DS
England

(Pr)

Theodore Presser Company
Presser Place
Bryn Mawr, PA 19010

(Thompson)

Gordon V. Thompson, Ltd.
29 Birch Avenue
Toronto, Ontario, M4V 1E2
Canada

(WLP)

World Library Publications, Inc.
2145 Central Parkway
Cincinnati, OH 45124

Unison Settings

Composer	Title	Publisher and Number
Greiner, Allen	Communion Service	Pr 312-40978
Hughes, Howard	San Jose Mass	GIA G-2063 (543-F)
Hurd, David	Intercession Mass	GIA G-2259
Hurd, David	Music for Celebration	GIA G-2258
Hurford, Peter	The Holy Eucharist	Hinshaw HMC-265
Isele, David Clark	Sacred Heart Mass	GIA G-2013
Johnson, David	Hosanna (Folk Communion Service)	Augsburg 11-9227
Lee, John	Congregation Mass 1970	GIA G-1552 (495-F)
McCabe, Michael	Mass for the New Rite	Hinshaw HMC-193
Near, Gerald	Music for Eucharist	Calvary Press

Forces Required	Notes	Portions of Texts Set
Unison	Congregational parts available, easy	K,G,S
Unison & cantor	Latin style, opt. percussion	K,G,S,Ac,Am,LP,AD
Unison choir with descants, cong., organ, opt. brass	Moderately difficult organ, skillfully written—the elegant "New York sound"	K,G,S,LP,AD,Xp
Unison choir with descants, cong., organ, opt. brass	Elegant, inspired, very singable, organ moderately difficult	K,G,S,LP,Xp
Unison & organ	Simplistic	K,G,Cr,S,Ac,LP, Xp,AD
Cantor, cong., organ	Moderately easy	G,S,Ac,AD
Cong. & organ (and/or guitar)	Easy	K,Tr,G,Cr,S,Ac, LP,AD,Xp
Unison	Chant style, easy	K,G,S,AD
Unison, with descants	Easy, skillfully written	K,G,Tr,S,Xp,LP,AD
Unison	Moderately difficult	K(2),G,S,AD

(continued)

Unison Settings *(continued)*

Composer	Title	Publisher and Number
Proulx, Richard	A New Mass	GIA G-2288
Robinson, McNeil	Music for the Lord's Supper	Pr 312-41263
Wyton, Alec	A People's Eucharist	Hope A449
Plainsong	Festal Mass of St. Mary	Comm. St. Mary
Plainsong	Light & Life	Comm. St. Mary

Forces Required	Notes	Portions of Texts Set
Unison with descants, cong., organ	Easy	K,T,G(2),S,Ac,Am, AD,Xp
Unison & organ	Very singable, useful	K,G,S,LP,Xp,AD
Unison	Creed is older ICET version, not BCP, difficult for cong.	K,Tr,G,Cr,S,AD,LP,Xp
Unison	Missa Marialis	K,G,Cr,S,Xp,AD
Unison	Plainsong for Paschaltide	G,S,Ac,Xp,AD

Settings for Congregation and Choir, etc.

Composer	Title	Publisher and Number
Arnatt, Ronald	Gloria & Sanctus	GIA G-1987
della Picca, Angelo	Mass of Hope	WLP CC-2078
Dello Joio, Norman	Mass in honor of BVM	AMP A-718
Diettrich, Philip	Communion Service	Agape AG 7181
Ferris, William	Missa Papae Septembris	GIA G-2286
Gelineau, Joseph	Festival Mass	B&H 5922
Goemanne, Noel	English Mass for 2 voices	GIA G-1551 (494-F)
Goemanne, Noel	Mass for SAB	GIA G-1571 (507-F)
Hallock, Peter	Trisagion & Gloria	GIA A-2187/2188
Hampton, Calvin	Mass for the New Rite	GIA G-1988 (539-F)

Forces Required	Notes	Portions of Texts Set
Cong. & opt. SATB	Moderately easy	G,S
Cong. & SAB	Easy	K,G,S,AD
Cantor, cong., 3-part choir	Large scale work; organ & opt. brass	K,G,S,AD
Unison or 2-part & cantor	Folk-style, creed is older ICET version, not BCP	K,Tr,G,Cr,AD,LP,Xp
Cong., SATB, organ	Moderately difficult	K,G,S,Ac,Am,LP,AD
Cong. & unison or SATB choir	Cong. parts available	K,G,S,AD
Cong., cantor & 2-part choir	Opt. flute or oboe	K,G,S,AD
Cong., cantor & SAB	Opt. brass & tympani, medium difficulty	K,G,S,AD
Cong., SATB, organ (opt. trumpet and handbells)	Moderately difficult, easy cong. parts, interesting rhythmic idiom	Tr,G
Cong. & opt. SATB	Medium difficulty for cong., very difficult organ part. Creed is older ICET version, not BCP	K,Tr,G,Cr,S,Ac,LP(2), AD,Xp

(continued)

Settings for Congregation and Choir, etc. *(continued)*

Composer	Title	Publisher and Number
Holman, Derek	The Niagara Mass	Thompson G-593 (G-593a)
Hovhaness, Alan	Simple Mass, Op. 282	Assoc A-727
Isele, David C.	The Notre Dame Mass	GIA G-1908 (533-F)
King, Larry	Missa Archangelis	GIA G-2126
Kreutz, Robert	Mass for an American Saint	WLSM CC-7537
McLin, Lena	Eucharist of the Soul	GWM
Nelhybel, Vaclav	Sanctus in D Minor	GIA G-2091
Peloquin, Alexander	Mass of the Bells	GIA G-1808
Proulx, Richard	Carillon Mass	GIA G-2067 (542-F)
Proulx, Richard	Carillon Mass	GIA G-2237

Forces Required	Notes	Portions of Texts Set
Cong. & opt. SATB	Opt. brass, moderately difficult	K,G,S(no Ben),Ac,AD
Cong. & SATB or unison choir	Moderately difficult	K,G,Cr,S,AD
SATB, cong., cantor & organ	Easy	K,Tr,G,S,Ac,AD,Xp
Cong. & SATB choir	Opt. instruments up to full rock ensemble, cong. part available	K,G,S,LP
Cong., SATB, organ	Easy, flowing, Southern folk-hymn style	K,G,S,AD
Cong. & SATB with piano	Soul style	K,Tr,G,Cr,S,LP,AD,Xp
SATB, cong. & organ	Easy cong. part, opt. brass & tympani	S,Am (only)
SATB, cong., cantor, & organ	Moderately difficult choir, easy cong. part	K,G,S,Ac,Am,AD
Cantor, cong., SATB	Handbells & percussion	K,G,S,Ac,Am,AD
Cantor, cong., SATB	Same as above, but bells replaced by flute & organ	K,G,S,Ac,Am,AD

(continued)

Settings for Congregation and Choir etc. *(continued)*

Composer	Title	Publisher and Number
Proulx, Richard	A Community Mass	GIA G-1605 (509-F)
Proulx, Richard	A Festival Eucharist	GIA G-1960 (538-F)
Proulx, Richard	Mass of the Redeemer	GIA G-1749
Proulx, Richard	Song of the Angels	GIA G-1996
Smith, Robert E.	Festive Liturgy	GIA G-2112 (547-F)
Tuuk, Jonathan	Mass of the Holy Trinity	GIA G-2103
Tuuk, Jonathan	Mass of St. Andrew	GIA G-2192
Wills, Arthur	Mass for the Seminary of the Southwest	Hinshaw
Wyton, Alec	For All the People	Gem GP-412/502

Forces Required	Notes	Portions of Texts Set
Cantor, cong., opt. SATB, or 3 equal voices	Opt. brass, percussion or strings, cong. part easy	K,G,S,Ac,Am,AD,Xp
Cong., SATB	Easy cong., choir medium difficulty	S,Ac,Am,AD (S,AD pub. sep.)
Cong., SATB	Brass & percussion ad lib, easy	K,Tr,G,S,Ac,AD,Xp
Cong. & 2 voices	Bells & percussion, medium difficulty	G only
Cong., SATB	Choir & organ, medium difficulty, cong. part easy	K,G,S(2),Ac(2), Am(2),AD
SATB & organ	Cong. part on S only, moderately easy	K,G,S,Am,Ac,AD
Cong., SATB, organ (handbells, brass, tympani ad lib)	Well-crafted, easy cong. part	K,G,S,Ac,Am,AD
Unison cong. or choir	Difficult, but SI easy, both LP texts set (both easy)	K,Tr,G,Cr,S(2),LP(2), AD
Cong., SATB, brass, tympani, bells, organ	Moderately easy, festive, cong. parts available	K,G,Tr,S,LP(2),Xp, Ac(3),AD

Series Three (Church of England) Settings *(See note in introductory material*

Composer	Title	Publisher and Number
Aston, Peter	Holy Communion	RSCM-123
Barrett-Ayres, Reginald	Communion Service	Nov MW 22
Dearnley & Wicks	Communion Service	OUP S604 (AS325)
Gibbs, Alan	St. Margaret's Comm.	RSCM 122 (122a)
Hesford, Bryan	Missa in Simplicitate	RSCM: Cramer 24
Hubbard & Cocking	The Salisbury Setting	Mayhew-McCrimmon
Hurford, Peter	Communion Service	Nov MW 28
Mathias, William	Communion Service	OUP S611 (S611a)
Rutter, John	Communion Service	OUP S598
Sharp, Ian	St. Katherine's Communion Service	Stainer & Bell CS 360 (Galaxy)

Forces Required	Notes	Portions of Texts Set
Cong., SATB, organ	First rate! Moderately easy	K,G,S,Ac,AD
Cantor, cong., organ	Moderately easy, interesting construction based on 3 unusual motifs, very singable	K,G,Cr,S,AD
Unison, opt. SATB	Quasi-plainsong	K,G,S,Ac(2),Fr,LP,AD
Cong./choir unison	Opt. SATB, medium difficulty	K,G,S,Ac(2),AD
Cantor, cong., organ	Quasi-plainsong, moderately easy	K,G,S,Ac,AD
Unison	Cong. part available	K,G,S,Ac(2),LP,AD
Double: Cong./choir	Choirs SATB & SB, difficult	K,G,S,Ac(2),LP,AD
Unison, opt. SATB	Moderately difficult accomp., easy voices	K,G,S,Ac(2),AD
Unison, opt. SATB	First rate! Cong. part available	K,G,S,Ac(2),AD
Unison (cong.) & organ (or guitar or piano)	Very easy, especially attractive G	K,G,S,Ac,AD

(continued)

Series Three (Church of England) Settings *(continued)*

Composer	Title	Publisher and Number
Shepard, Richard	The Addington Service	RSCM 121
Shepard, Richard	The Wiltshire Service	RSCM 126
Walker, Robert	Communion Service in E	Nov MW 40
Plainsong	Missa de Angelis	St. Mary's Press

Forces Required	Notes	Portions of Texts Set
Unison	Opt. SATB in AD only, easy	K,G,S,Ac(2),AD
Opt. cong., SATB, organ	Easy writing in familiar style, impractical cong. part	K,G,S,Ac,AD
Unison	Medium difficulty	K,G,S,Ac(2),LP,AD
Unison	Plainsong notation	K(3),G,Cr,S,Ac, LP(2),AD

Choral Settings without Congregational Parts

Composer	Title	Publisher and Number
Davye, John	Missa Brevis	Assoc A-714
Fauré, Gabriel	Mass	Pr 312-41006
Hancock, Gerre	Missa Resurrectionis	OUP 94.213
Jackson, Francis	Comm. Service, Series 3	OUP CMS 05
Jenkins, Joseph W.	Mass in Tudor Modes	EV 362-03198
Kelly, Bryan	Comm. Service, Series 3	OUP CMS 06
Sr. Maria of the Cross	Mass for Peace	OUP 94.005
Moore, Philip	Holy Communion, Series 3	Addington Press, RSCM
Proulx, Richard	Gloria for a Holy Day	GIA G-2287
Wills, Arthur	Missa in Memoriam Benjamin Britten, Series 3	Addington Press, RSCM

Forces Required	Notes	Portions of Texts Set
SATB unaccomp.	Latin & English, moderately easy	K,G,S,AD
SATB & organ (originally 2-voices)	Easy, English, French, Latin	K,S,AD
SATB & organ	Moderately easy	K,G,S,AD
SATB & organ	Moderately easy	K,G,S,AD
SAB & organ	Choral parts moderately difficult	K,G,S,AD
SATB & organ	Moderately difficult choir, organ part difficult	K,G,S,AD
2 voices & organ	Easy	K,G,S,AD
SATB & organ	Difficult	K,G,S,Ac,AD
SATB & string quartet	Easy, opt. fl, tri, brass, organ	G only
SATB & organ	Difficult	K,G,S,AD